PLANT MAGIC

for the

Beginner
Witch

PLANT MAGIC

for the

Beginner Witch

An Herbalist's Guide to Heal, Protect and Manifest

ALLY SANDS

Founder of Aquarian Soul

PAGE STREET
PUBLISHING CO.

PAGE STREET
PUBLISHING CO.

dedication

To all the witches who came before me.
Thank you for opening the path.

TABLE *of* CONTENTS

abundance . . . 81

INTRODUCTION

I am a witch, and I am an herbalist. These two often go hand in hand, and many might argue that they are very much the same thing. I come from a long line of plant healers, including my second great-grandfather who was a well-known and respected *curandero* (healer) in my mom's hometown. He had an entire handwritten book full of his recipes, which unfortunately was given away. Most of my maternal side of the family sees and hears spirits and has a strong belief in *brujeria* (witchcraft) and *yerberos* (herbalists). I have always felt this innate pull to work with plants and work with the elements to create my own reality—and apparently, it's in my blood.

We all have different opinions and experiences in life that lead us down the path that we're currently on. All the spells and opinions in this book are my own interpretations. I might not hold the same ideas a lot of other witches do—and maybe you don't either. Maybe you don't really fit into one box and you want to carve your own path, and that's totally okay!

A lot of people like strict directions and guidance, but the best guide is yourself. I can't tell you that my spells will or won't work for you. It's what you believe, and it's the energy and effort that you put into it. If buying expensive ingredients and making your own tools by hand makes you feel happy and brings you a sense of power, then go for it. If all you have access to are candles from the dollar store and a bottle of dried basil from your parent's spice rack, that doesn't make the magic any less potent or any less real for you.

All the magic you have is within you. You don't need to read any books or do any deep diving in the occult and ceremonial magic. You don't have to go to some secret, members-only occultist shop with dusty shelves and bottles of potions and dried herbs to get obscure books and ingredients. All you really need is your own self-determination and some ingredients you could probably find at your grocery store.

Don't let me tell you who you need to be and don't let anyone else tell you who you need to be. Part of the magical allure of being a witch is that you create your own craft. You are guided by your own inner compass. If I could tell you one thing it would be to throw away all your spell books because you don't really need them. But then again, would I be writing this book if that were the truth? Of course you need some guidelines to get started, but YOU are the key ingredient to your magic workings.

Life itself is magic. You work with the moon cycles, with the changing seasons, with flowers and herbs—with nature itself. Every single moment is an opportunity to celebrate the magic around us. Making tea becomes a ceremony. Taking a bath becomes a ritual. You appreciate the small things around you so that you can be one with the divine.

The concept of magic is not as esoteric as one might think. Every day we create the day ahead in our minds before it happens. Every thought we have can affect our outer world. Witchcraft simply adds tools and words of power to bring these inner thoughts into our outer reality. This is what magic is. You add ingredients or say certain chants or do specific gestures because you feel it will work. It is all within you to create change in your life. Trust in your intuition and trust in your own power.

This book introduces basic guidelines for the beginner witch. I use traditional herbs, magical herbs and a couple of more common plants that you can probably find on your morning walk or a trip to your local nursery. I attempted to use a lot of herbs that overlap within the different chapters of this book so that you can try a lot of the spells without having to buy a million ingredients.

It is my hope that you are able to use the rituals presented in this book to help you explore your own inner power. You have the capability to bring love, abundance and good health into your life. Throughout this book you will learn how to harness this energy and create the life you desire, using simple herbs and spices you can find almost anywhere. So if you want to learn about earth magic, green witchcraft and how to incorporate herbs into your practice from an unconventional Aquarius witch, read on.

what is a spell?

A spell is a form of ritual to enact positive change in your life. You use tools and your intentions on the physical realm to manifest change in other realms. We are all energy: you, me, crystals, herbs, everything around us. As the laws of physics state, you can neither create nor destroy energy. You are merely using your thoughts and intent to redistribute energy. Transform it to create the reality you want for yourself. Much like prayer, or "sending good vibes" to someone, you are in essence using your own inner power and intent to change things in your favor. You are transforming your world to how you would like to see it. We all do this unconsciously every day.

Doing spells does not mean that you won't have to put in work. Raising energy, focusing your mind and carrying the spell through involves effort and energy. You are the catalyst for directing the energies. You, in essence, are the main ingredient in a spell. Once the spell is cast, you still need to keep focused, stay positive and work toward your intention. You can't cast a spell for finding a job or bringing in more money, then sit on the couch all day. You must do your part.

Results don't happen overnight. They can, but most likely it will take some time. Time on this physical plane is linear, but with magic we understand time as existing all at once. We work with the past, the present and the future. What you want to happen is already happening on a different dimension or on a different wavelength. But since we are working with the energies present here on this dimension, things work more slowly than our minds are capable of creating. This is a dense, slow-moving energy on this planet.

Having a spell work quickly also involves a lot of belief. Trusting that things will work out the way you want them is key. Once you do the spell, forget about it. You have given your intentions to the universe, and what you desire is on its way to you. If you keep obsessing or thinking about it, you are slowing it down. Trust in yourself, in your power. Believe that what you want will come in perfect timing.

working with the elements

Some of you might already be familiar with the pentagram. It represents the elements: earth, air, fire, water and spirit. But what do the elements mean in the context of witchcraft? We use them all in spells, as representations on the altar, when casting a circle and even as foods we eat.

Water and earth are receptive elements. Water can be represented by any liquid. When you drink wine or tea, make a potion, collect rainwater—all of these are represented by the element of water. Any solid object such as a candle, a metal tray, a bowl of salt or crystals, these are all representations of earth. They are receptive and capable of absorbing energy. They are used to take on the properties and intentions you give them. This is why we program crystals to work for us. This is why we can make potions for love or success. The liquids and solids take on the energy that we use to do our spells.

Air and fire release energy. Air can be represented by incense, sage wands, bells and any kind of smoke. When we burn herbs, resins or incense, we are in essence releasing the energy out into the universe. Fires can be made in your cauldron and whatever they touch will be released from you.

This is why magic is so potent. The elements around us help us manifest our desires through absorbing and releasing energy. The very forms that make up life itself. We are inextricably linked to the elements around us. Our own bodies are composed of water and a variety of elements. So whatever change we make with the use of elements has an effect on our physical reality. We create our own reality, with the help of the elements.

harnessing your energy

But how do you harness this energy? What if you have doubts about the situation, will it still work? There are three important factors when doing magic: having the right intention, being able to focus and putting your energy into a spell.

Decide on your intention. Do you want to bring in a constant flow of money from your business? Or do you simply need a specific amount of money to pay off a bill? You don't want to do a spell without a clear and concise intention. Do you want to find a penny on the ground tomorrow? My guess is no, and you need to clearly state that. Think it. Speak it aloud. Write it on a piece of paper. Carve it into a candle, or scream it into the universe. However you need to get it across, make sure you have an intention in mind before starting.

Focus your energy. Worries, doubts and insecurities can make it hard to focus all our positive energy into our goal. You need to know that whatever you desire is possible; you just need to believe in it. Meditation can be a helpful tool when working on your focus. To perform magic, you need to clear out all the chatter in your mind. Never go into a spell if you are feeling doubtful, sad or confused. You need to know that your will and your strength can bring your manifestations to fruition.

Spend ten minutes every day practicing meditation. You can even do it right before you do a spell. Let go of old ideas and patterns of how "the world works" or how a person is "just that way" or how your fate is somehow sealed. We are all capable of change, growth and evolution. Clear your mind and know exactly what you want. That is all you need. Don't worry about how it will come to you, just trust that it's on its way.

Direct your energy. You might be asking how exactly do I put energy into something? What does it mean to raise energy and put it into your rituals? Well, have you ever listened to a song and felt emotion build up inside of you? Have you ever been in a crowd of people at a concert or a gathering with strong positive, happy energy and your body felt electric? There is energy within you that you can use in order to propel a spell forward.

For example, if your intention is to be married, think of the person that you want to be with. How does it make you feel? Happy? Overjoyed? When you are doing a spell, focus on those positive feelings you will have when you are together in a happy relationship with that person. Let the emotion overtake you and build inside of you. Imagine that energy building to a high point, then direct it through visualization, moving your body or dancing. Push the energy into the spell, then release it and it will return to you in the form of your manifestation.

Do this with any form of magic. If you want protection, imagine yourself relaxed, calm and surrounded by a bright white light. If you want to do a spell for personal power, then dance, sing or chant. Let the energy rise inside of you so that you can feel strong and energetic. Do whatever makes that energy really vibrate within you.

a word on wildcrafting

Many herbalists have learned that wildcrafting or foraging for herbs is a time-honored tradition and one of the best ways to learn about herbs. As we grow, we adapt to new ways of thinking. There are many plants, such as white sage, that are at risk of being endangered because of humans. We overharvest plants and even harvest during the wrong time of year.

Plants were here long before us. They can take care of themselves. They have their seasons to grow, to endure and to flourish. When we interfere with this natural cycle, we are disrupting an entire ecosphere. You really don't know if the plants had a bad year unless you are present for these cycles. Be aware that even if you are observing the plants carefully, you may be on someone else's land and taking the plants may be illegal.

I have lived in Southern California my entire life. I see the various native plants around me year after year. I see the effect that the drought had on the plants. This year was the first year in a long time that I have seen the white sage stands looking healthy. I have refrained from harvesting in the wild for a while now, and have refocused on growing nearly 95 percent of what we use in our products in our own medicinal garden.

Appreciate plants when you go out into nature, and don't pick them unless you really know what you are doing. If you want to use plants that you find in the wild make sure they are prolific and aren't endangered. Watch the land they grow on through the seasons. Only take a small piece, only what you need for the spell or a small handful to store for later use.

Some of the plants mentioned in these spells aren't as easily found in a store, but foraging for these ingredients isn't harmful because none of these plants are endangered and you will only be using a leaf or two in some cases. Some examples include magnolia flowers, passionflower or strawberry leaves. You can certainly find these at a garden center, from a neighbor's tree, a sidewalk planting strip, an alleyway or even reaching over the fence in a parking lot or apartment complex. I like to call this urban foraging. Once you get to know plants better you will start noticing them everywhere.

Below is a list of magical herbs you can try growing yourself. You can create your own witch garden!

Aloe Vera	Hibiscus	Sage
Basil	Hyssop	St. John's wort
Calendula	Lavender	Thyme
Chamomile	Lemon Verbena	Vervain
Comfrey	Rose	Yarrow
Dill	Rosemary	
Feverfew	Rue	

These herbs spread quite a bit or require more space. Keep these in pots if you have limited space, so they don't overtake your entire gardening space.

Angelica
Bay (Prune it to keep it a manageable size.)
Jasmine (vining)
Lemon balm
Mint

Mugwort (Keep it in a pot at all costs. Seeds will spread and take over every part of your yard.)
Passionflower (This vining plant needs a trellis or fence to climb.)

a word on white sage

Many witches and people in the spiritual community use white sage for purification during rituals. It is sold at every new age store, health food store and everywhere online. If you know anything about me or my company, you know that I have been advocating for growing your own sage for years. White sage is considered an at-risk plant in the wild. It is being overharvested by big companies in its native habitat. There are very few farms that grow sage for commercial use. We are slowly waking up to this and a couple of farms are popping up, but the majority of sage comes from the wild.

It's important to keep in mind that white sage grows in such a small area, and we are already encroaching on its native habitat. We are building over irreplaceable desert landscape and putting strain on animal and plant populations with new housing projects and highways, not to mention natural devastation from fires and drought. The plant just can't survive forever with us adding to the problem.

White sage is also a sacred plant to many Native American tribes. I strongly encourage you to find out more about your ancestry and work with plants that correspond with your own traditions. It is also a good idea not to refer to cleansing with herbs as "smudging" as that is specific to Native people. Instead choose words like purifying, cleansing or ritual herbs.

As green witches, as people who love the earth and everything on it, we need to be mindful of the ingredients we use. Things need to change. If you do want to use white sage, try growing it yourself from seed or buy a small plant. White sage can grow in many climates. There are also many accessible and sustainable substitutes for white sage. Try rosemary, lavender, cedar, even resins such as frankincense and copal. There are hundreds of varieties of sage you can try growing yourself to make wands from; even the common culinary sage will work!

If you buy white sage, find a Native American vendor. And remember, white sage is a potent, resinous plant, so a little goes a very long way. You only need a single leaf to cleanse yourself and your space. The amount of sage I have seen end up at discount stores, flea markets and even gas stations for a couple of dollars is just sad. Large bundles aren't necessary, and there is no need to buy a large quantity of an at-risk plant. Give respect to the land we live on, and always ask the plant for permission to use it.

PROTECTION

Days: Saturday and Tuesday
Moon Phase: full moon, new moon or waning moon
Colors: black, dark purple and red

Are you an empath? A highly sensitive person? Are you in tune with the barrage of energies whizzing around you on a daily basis? Then this section is definitely for you. When you are open and receptive, you can take on a lot of negativity from the people around you. You can feel physically or emotionally ill. Empaths have the tendency to attract energy vampires: people who really drain you, whether they mean to or not. As I can relate to this, I created this section so you learn to protect yourself from any incoming energy that can harm you.

Every witch should have protection spells in her arsenal. This chapter will cover many different kinds of spells to help you protect your energy. In a rare event of a psychic attack or actual hexing or cursing, you will know how to protect yourself. In general, protection spells are more for everyday use to help you set boundaries, protect your own energy from negative people or protect your home and those you love.

The herbs often used for protection spells are sage, rosemary, mugwort, juniper, lavender, cedar and angelica. Every culture has specific herbs that are used for protection, but some of these are universal.

Sage is an herb that many associate with protection and cleansing. There are hundreds of varieties of sage that you can use, including culinary sage. This is easy to find and sustainable. Sage may be burned in a dried bundle or as a loose incense, or kept on you as part of a spell. Carry a leaf in your pocket to ward off negative energies.

Rosemary is a bit of an all-purpose herb in magic. One of its primary uses is for protection. It has powerful cleansing properties that help you rid yourself and your space of negativity. It is one of the most ancient forms of incense. It is often hung from your home to aid in protection of its inhabitants. Add a few drops of essential oil into a spray bottle full of water to spray whatever you want to protect.

Mugwort is a magical herb. It is used in dreamwork, divination and protection. To aid in protection during astral projection, meditation or magic workings, place mugwort under your pillow, use it on your altar or keep it with you during a spell. A dried mugwort bundle can be hung near your bed or burned to purify and protect you.

Juniper can be used for both its berries and for the leaves. It is a fiery herb ruled by the sun. It can also be burned to protect your space. A branch hung by the door protects your home from evil and negative energies. If you don't have access to juniper's foliage, you can boil the berries and use the steam in the same way to protect your home. Plant a juniper near your front or back door to protect from thieves.

Lavender is another multipurpose herb. It carries the element of air which makes it great for purification and protection in the form of smoke. In this section, we will be using lavender smoke to purify and protect your home. It can also be used in protection baths, amulets and pretty much any spell.

Cedar is a protective herb that is used across many cultures. It is a sustainable alternative to white sage. It is commonly used by Native Americans as a ceremonial herb for purification. In magical use, cedar drives away negative or harmful spirits. Cedar can be worn as a charm or talisman to protect you on your journey.

Angelica is used for its leaves, flowers and roots. It is also known as archangel for its protective properties. Sprinkle dried angelica leaves in the four corners of your home or around the perimeter to ward off negative energy. Use it in talismans, amulets and herbal bath preparations to remove any spell work done against you.

COPAL AND QUARTZ PROTECTIVE SPRAY

Making a spray is a great way to harness the protective powers of herbs without needing to burn anything. This spray can go with you in your bag, on your nightstand or in your car, so you have it everywhere you go. It's perfect for situations where burning incense or an herbal bundle is not practical or may even be dangerous. Just ask me about the time an out-of-control sage bundle set off my fire alarm and the fire department showed up! I like to energize these sprays with the addition of crystals and salt. Salt is a highly protective ingredient for witches that dispels negative energy and creates an energetic boundary around us. Think of this as a protective shield for when you are out in the world interacting with people.

ingredients
Mortar and pestle

3 star anise

1 tbsp (5 g) myrrh

1 tbsp (6 g) copal

7 juniper berries or 3 drops juniper essential oil

3 pieces of cedar or 3 drops cedar essential oil

Small jar with a lid

3 pieces of fresh lemon peel

½ cup (120 ml) vodka

Rainwater

1 black tourmaline

1 clear quartz

2 tsp (12 g) sea salt

1 (4-oz [120-ml]) spray bottle

the ritual

Before you put the spray together, you have to infuse your herbs in vodka for a few weeks. This is the same process used to make tinctures in herbalism. Tinctures are herbal infusions made with alcohol to be taken as oral supplements. This process is used to extract the oils, waxes, minerals, vitamins—most of the plant materials. This will also impart the scent of all the plants into the spray. If we were to put it directly into the water, there would hardly be any scent. If you want to just use water, you can use all essential oils instead of the whole plant.

To release the fragrant oils and to break them down, you use your mortar to crush them. These don't need to be a powder; but the more surface area exposed to the alcohol, the better it will infuse. Grind each herb one by one in your mortar. Call upon each herb to help you provide protection. As you do this, place each crushed herb into a small jar. Also add in your lemon peel. Once your herbs are in the jar, fill it to the top with vodka. Cover the jar and let this sit for a full moon cycle.

During a rainstorm, catch some rainwater for use in this spell. If it isn't a rainy season, keep rainwater in a jar to use later or use ocean water or the most natural source you can find. If you live near a spring, use that. If you have a stream near your house, gather water from there. If all you have is purified water, that's fine too!

Place your crystals and salt into your spray bottle. Strain the herbs that have been steeping for a month out of the alcohol. Fill your spray bottle with the alcohol, and top with the water. If you have leftover alcohol, you can keep it as the mother batch to refill your bottle with or to give away to friends and family.

Once your bottle is ready, set it on your workspace and charge it. You can do this by leaving it overnight in the moonlight, with a candle, incense smoke or any method that feels instinctually right to you. Then it is ready to use.

HYSSOP PROTECTION OIL

Hyssop is a wonderful herb for protection, purification and cleansing. It is an ancient herb that's mentioned in a lot of early magical books. You won't find this herb at your corner store, but you can find hyssop online, in herb stores or in witchy shops. It's in the mint family so you can easily grow it yourself as well. It aids in protecting you from any negative energies that may be sticking to you. This oil combines hyssop with other protective herbs, and it will work for a multitude of purposes. I love making oils so much because you can use them for almost anything. I suggest you leave this to steep for a full moon cycle before using it.

ingredients

Protection incense
Small jar with a lid
3 tbsp (15 g) dried hyssop
3 tbsp (21 g) frankincense
3 tbsp (10 g) dried rosemary
3 tbsp (6 g) dried sage
3 tbsp (6 g) dried mugwort
3 star anise
3 cloves
1 bay leaf
1 cinnamon stick or 1 tbsp (8 g) cinnamon chips
Optional: mortar and pestle
Pinch of sea salt
Sunflower or other plant-based oil
1 small black candle

the ritual

Light your favorite protection incense to set the mood. Try rosemary, cloves, cinnamon or bay. Clean your jar on the outside and inside by holding it over your incense. Set your intention for this oil. What will you need protection from? Is this for a specific purpose or an all-around protection? Close your eyes and visualize a bubble of protection around you.

Begin adding each herb one by one. You can break them into smaller pieces or lightly crush them in your mortar to release the fragrance. As you place them in the jar, whisper over each herb "protect me" or "thank you for protecting me." It is always good to show gratitude to the plants that are working for us. Add in your pinch of salt. When all the ingredients are in your jar, fill it to the top with oil and cover it with a lid.

Inscribe the candle with the word "protection" or with symbols or words that represent protection to you. Always make it personal to your intention. Light the candle and let it burn. You can do this over the jar or next to it. I always like to do it over the jar so the wax drips down, but it's up to you! Let this sit for a full moon cycle before using it. When it's ready, use this to anoint candles, other spell work, yourself, others, your home or your car.

CEDAR PROTECTIVE
HERB BUNDLE

Many shops sell white sage or cedar bundles, but it is not often you see other herbs in a wand. Cedar has the same cleansing and protective properties as sage; and this bundle makes a wonderful alternative to white sage. If you want to add in your favorite herbs, that's fantastic. Or try using only pine, lavender and rosemary. Substitute the cedar, if it's hard to find. Make this your own: the more of your own beliefs and energy you can add into these tools, the better.

ingredients
Optional: charcoal disc and white candles
5 cedar branches
5 eucalyptus branches
5 sprigs of fresh rosemary
3 roses or a handful of petals
5–7 lavender stems
1–3 cinnamon sticks
1 (72-inch [1.8-m]) piece of red string

the ritual

Make this bundle on a Tuesday. This is a great day for making any kind of protective tools or doing protection spells. If you like, light any of the herbs listed in the ingredients on your charcoal disc and light some white candles.

Begin by laying down the cedar. Take off any of the thicker, woodier stems. Lay them on top of each other forming the base of this bundle. Then add your eucalyptus, then rosemary. Shape the bundle between your hands, squeezing it together to get everything in place. Lastly you will add your roses, lavender and cinnamon.

Fold the string in half and place the bundle over the center point of the string. Holding the bundle together tightly with one hand, begin to wrap the string in a crisscross pattern starting with the top and moving your way down to the base of the bundle. Once you reach the bottom, wrap the string around a few times and tie it off.

When the bundle is finished, lay your hands over the herbs, charging it with your intentions for protection. Let your bundle dry for about 2 weeks before using it. You will know when it's completely dry when the herbs snap to the touch.

Use this bundle for almost anything. Burn this before spells or during spells, or use it to cleanse your home, yourself or someone else. You can even make a few to share. This is a good way to give gifts friends and family can appreciate even if they don't hold the same beliefs.

RAINBOW FLOWER AURA CLEANSING RITUAL

We use colors to affect change in all areas of our lives, including magic. We use different colored candles for spell work or to lift our spirits. Color can change the energy and even cleanse our aura. Each one of our chakras is associated with one of the colors of the rainbow. When we use the entire visible spectrum of color, we are unifying all the different energetic systems within the body. Light is deeply healing and regenerating. By aligning your energetic body you bring a balance to the flow of energy in your body. You feel well physically and mentally. This ritual helps dissolve any imbalances within, and it helps activate any blocked energy centers. You can do this ritual on yourself, but it's also great to do with a partner! We will use the color properties of herbs; if you feel drawn to an herb of the same color that's not on this list, use whatever calls to you.

ingredients

1 tbsp (3 g) dried lavender

1 tbsp (2 g) dried hibiscus

1 tbsp (2 g) dried cornflower

1 tbsp (2 g) dried lemon balm

1 tbsp (2 g) dried chamomile

1 tbsp (2 g) dried calendula

1 tbsp (2 g) dried rose petals

7 small jars with lids

1 clear quartz crystal

1 amethyst crystal

1 amazonite crystal

1 jade crystal

1 citrine crystal

1 tiger's eye crystal

1 carnelian crystal

Sunflower or other plant-based oil

the ritual

As this ritual is based on color, I have chosen all herbs and crystals for their color correspondences. The heart center is represented by the color green even though there are many pink stones correlated to the heart such as rose quartz.

To begin you will infuse your oil with your herbs and crystals. You will be making seven separate oils. You will be using only small quantities of these oils so use the smallest jars you can find.

Place each herb one by one in your hand. Cup your other hand around the herbs and enchant them. Imagine the color of the herb glowing a bright light. If you are enchanting the lavender, imagine a light purple light emanating from the lavender. Let it grow slowly until it encompasses your entire hand. Do this for about 1 minute per herb. Imagine each herb working in unison to align your body. Feel the balance, and free-flowing energy within your body. Place the herbs into the jars along with the corresponding crystal: lavender/clear quartz, hibiscus/amethyst, cornflower/amazonite, lemon balm/jade, chamomile/citrine, calendula/tiger's eye, rose petals/carnelian.

Fill each jar to the top with oil and cover it with a lid. Let these oils infuse for at least 3 days before performing this ritual. The longer you let the herbs sit, the richer and more aromatic they will become. The energetic properties will remain the same after 3 days. Set up a cozy area with blankets, or lie down on your couch or bed. Light some candles and incense. Set the mood that makes you feel most relaxed. Lay out your jars alongside you. It is helpful if you have a partner to perform this on each other. If you are alone, line the jars up in order of chakras alongside your body so you can easily reach over to them with your eyes still closed.

To begin, lie down and close your eyes. Take a few deep breaths. Starting from your base chakra, apply some of the corresponding oil to your hands. Rub your hands together until they feel warm and you feel the energy building. Place your hands over that energy center and hold them there. Imagine the color red beginning to glow from your body. The red glowing light begins to spin and turn in a clockwise motion. It is spinning freely. Feel the energy beginning to rise up to the next chakra. Do this for each oil, until you reach your crown chakra. Place your hands on the top of your head or slightly above your head. Imagine a white light bursting out of the center of your head. Your entire body is illuminated with a rainbow of lights and you are totally free-flowing and open. There are no more blockages within your body.

PINE RESIN
PROTECTION DUST

Pine is a magical tree that is recognized for its abilities to purify and protect. It aids in raising your energy so that nothing can harm you. It gives you an inner strength and resilience to overcome any adversities. This protection dust protects your home, and it makes you stronger to take on anything that may try to harm you. You can use whatever species of pine is growing near you. Pine resin is also used to help treat wounds, acting as an antibacterial and anti-inflammatory to help protect your skin. So you know this works as protection both physically and magically. Copal transmutes negative energies, transforming them into positive ones. Lemongrass is also used for protection and purification, and it smells so amazing! Like the other powder recipes in this book, you can use this around your home, on candles and in other spells.

ingredients
1 red candle
Mortar and pestle
5 tbsp (75 ml) pine resin
5 tbsp (30 g) copal
5 tbsp (25 g) dried hyssop
5 tbsp (16 g) dried rosemary
5 tbsp (10 g) dried sage
5 tbsp (25 g) dried lemongrass powder
Small jar with a lid
1 black tourmaline stone

the ritual

To begin, light your red candle. Using your mortar and pestle, grind your pine resin and copal to a powder. Focus your intentions on protection, whether that's protecting your home, yourself or another person. Set these aside.

Add each remaining herb, one by one, and grind them as finely as possible. You can find lemongrass powder online, as it won't break down as easily into a powder by hand.

Once you have all your herbs powdered, place them into your jar. Add the black tourmaline. You can pass the jar a few times over the flame of the candle, imagining yourself protected by a white light. No one can enter your sphere to harm you. You are safe, you are protected. You can chant these words aloud as you pass your powder through the flame.

Store this powder covered in the jar. Use this powder to anoint candles, on yourself, in other rituals or around your home so that no harm can enter.

HIGH VIBRATIONAL
LAVENDER HOUSE CLEANSE

Protecting your home and your space is of vital importance. This technique is something that I don't see often in other spells. Typically, when doing ritual cleansings, I like to open all the windows to allow everything out of the house. In this case you hold the smoke inside for a period of time to collect all the stagnant, negative energies, then you release them all at once. This ritual requires only one herb, making it super easy to do. But easy does not mean less powerful! Lavender is a highly effective herb for drawing out negative energy, while imparting its delicate, sweet energy and protecting your home. It is a high vibrational flower that will collect and disperse negative energies.

ingredients
30–40 dried lavender stems
2- to 3-foot (61- to 91-cm) piece of white string
Large bowl
Water
½ cup (144 g) salt

the ritual

Go around your home and shut all the windows and doors, then open all your closets, drawers and cabinets. You want the smoke to permeate every corner of your home.

Take your lavender stems and bundle them together. Wrap your white string around the lavender, starting at the bottom and moving your way to the top. Once you are about 2 inches (5 cm) from the top, wind the string back down to the bottom and tie it off. Once you are done, fill the bowl halfway with water and add the salt. Place the bowl in the middle of your home.

Light the end of the lavender until it begins to smoke. Go around your house, room by room and let the smoke waft all over into every crevice. While you walk, repeat this chant:

> *Sweet and lovely lavender*
> *Cleanse my space*
> *Protect my home*

Once you have finished, open up all the windows and doors. Let the smoke out all at once. Take your bowl of water and throw the water out the back door into the soil. The earth transmutes all the negative energy, so you don't have to worry about throwing the water out far away from your home.

HERBS AND SALT SPACE PROTECTION

While many of the spells in this book are more open-ended for any kind of protection you are seeking, this one is meant to be used solely for your home. When you see clichéd representations of witches, you often see them creating a circle of salt. Salt is definitely one of the top tools to use for protection. It can be added to almost any spell, used in casting your circle or, in this case, to safeguard your home. Use this when moving into a new home, when you feel unsafe or when you simply want to keep out people with negative energies. Using charcoal or ashes along with salt in many folk traditions is considered "black salt" or "witches salt." This is my own version of the traditional recipe.

ingredients
Large bowl
4 cups (1.1 kg) salt
½ cup (16 g) dried sage (common, white, black, sagebrush)
½ cup (18 g) dried lavender
½ cup (16 g) dried angelica
½ cup (16 g) dried peppermint
1 tbsp (6 g) black pepper
3 tbsp (18 g) activated charcoal (or ash from a spell or fire)
Optional: 8 drops lavender and/or 8 drops sage essential oil
Large jar with a lid

the ritual

In your bowl, add your salt. You can use table salt, sea salt, Himalayan salt or anything you have. When you are using salt for protection, it's not as important to use a specific kind.

Take each herb in your hand and charge it. You can cup it in your hand or place your hands over it, however you choose. You can also say something aloud, whatever feels comfortable and natural to you. Crumble each herb in your hand, into the bowl. The more your work the herbs in your hands, the more energy you are infusing into it.

Grind the black pepper into the bowl. Add in the charcoal. You can mix the salt with your hands or with a spoon. If you want to add a little zing, add one or both of the essential oils.

Place your salt in a jar until you are ready to use it. For this ritual you will be using it around your home, so if you want to use it right away you definitely can.

When you want to use the salt, go outside your home and begin to create a border around the entire property. Make a line with your salt all the way around, creating a whole circle. If you live in an apartment, you can do this around the front door and your balcony. You can also add a small amount to each corner of your home. As you lay down the salt, imagine a protective bubble encasing your entire home. No one who wants to cause you harm can enter. You are protected.

BAY LAUREL
PENTAGRAM WREATH

In magical workings, trees are actual representations of "as above, so below." The roots ground the tree, while the branches reach high up into the sky to bring the divine energy down into the physical world. Trees can be mysterious, powerful, strong, delicate and ethereal. They can be portals into the magical world of fairies, plant devas and other mystical creatures. You can get lost in a forest with the light dappling through the branches, moss beneath your feet and the scent of decaying leaves and soil all around you. Choosing the tree for this wreath is one of the most important factors. Some trees that represent protection are oak, ash, birch and cedar among others. If you have a tree near you, look for fallen twigs and branches on your next walk. Even though you are using a premade wreath, the pentagram should be made of twigs from these trees.

ingredients
5 twigs from an oak, ash, birch or cedar tree
1 grapevine wreath
Floral wire or twine
Handful of fresh rosemary sprigs
Handful of fresh bay leaves
Handful of fresh sage
12–15 lavender stems
Hot glue gun, if needed

the ritual

Go for a walk. This is the perfect time to feel connected to nature. Whether you live in a city or out in the country, a walk through the forest, around your neighborhood or along local hiking trails is a chance to connect. If you feel comfortable, you can even remove your shoes and go barefoot. Walking barefoot grounds you to the earth. Look up, what kind of trees are in your area? Do you see any oak or birch trees? Collect 5 small branches, or large twigs. Choose them based on how large you want to make this wreath.

Lay your wreath on your working space. Measure your twigs across the wreath to make sure they are long enough. You can always trim longer ones. Lay them down in the shape of a star. Using floral wire or twine, wrap each point of the star so it doesn't move. Once it feels secure, you can attach it to the wreath using either floral wire or twine.

Lay down the herbs however you want across the wreath. It's important that the herbs are pliable so you can bend them. But if you have dried herbs you can attach them with a hot glue gun. Using wire will snap them. As you tie each herb onto your wreath, imagine a barrier of protection forming.

Your front door is the portal into your home. Placing this wreath on your door acts as a barrier to all unwanted energies, thieves and unwelcome guests.

CHARCOAL PROTECTION BATH

Charcoal is prized for its many different uses. If you have ever had a stomachache, you might have taken charcoal tablets. Charcoal is used in magic for banishing, purifying and protection. You can write with it, or use it in oils and candles or as part of a protective bath. My first time making this bath, I unintentionally created a beautiful grey vortex that made these lovely smoky swirls underwater. Since then, it's been one of my favorite rituals to do. You can find activated charcoal as a powder or in capsule form at a health food store. Charcoal also acts as a detoxifying agent for your skin, so make sure and rinse off any impurities after this bath.

ingredients

Small saucepan or pot

Water

3 sprigs of fresh rosemary

3 tbsp (9 g) dried lavender buds

3 sprigs of fresh peppermint

Large jar with a lid

½ cup (60 g) coconut milk powder

½ cup (146 g) sea salt

¼ cup (24 g) charcoal

Obsidian, black tourmaline, amethyst, clear quartz or smoky quartz stones (use one or all of these)

the ritual

For this ritual you are going to brew the herbs like a tea. You won't be putting them directly in the bath. This brings out more of their aroma and energetic constituents, and it allows you to focus more on your intentions during the brewing process.

Put the saucepan of water to boil. Add in your rosemary, lavender and peppermint. You can use fresh or dried but if you have fresh all the better. Envision what you need protection for as you drop each herb into the water. You can even say the words out loud: "Protect me. Protect my home. Protect my energy." Once the herbs are in the water, turn the temperature to low and let them steep for about 10 minutes. You can stir them or focus on them, but keep an eye on them. Strain the herbs out and set the tea to the side.

Heat 2 cups (480 ml) of water. In a large jar, add your coconut milk powder, salt and charcoal. Add hot water to dissolve them. You can even shake it up if you like.

Run your bath. Add your crystals inside the water or on the edge of the tub. Once your bath is full, pour in your tea. Slowly pour in your charcoal mixture, and watch the swirls form. Imagine a vortex of protection surrounding you. You are encased in a protective cocoon.

Soak in the bath for as long as you like. Concentrate on yourself feeling safe, protected and out of harm's way. No one can infiltrate the physical and emotional boundaries you are setting. You are protected.

ROSEMARY HERBAL FLOOR SWEEP

Sweeping is a traditional ritual performed in many branches of witchcraft. It is a method of absorbing energy and sweeping it outside. You can do this to remove any harmful or unwanted energies from your home. This will even work if there are people who visit you who leave you feeling drained or leave a lot of heavy energy in your space. You can find many recipes like this one, but this is my personal blend that I use in my home. It uses highly protective herbs, along with the most protective ingredient in any witch's collection—salt! This simple ritual only requires herbs and a little time.

ingredients
Large bowl

3 cups (876 g) salt (sea salt, Epsom or table salt),
more or less as needed

½ cup (26 g) dried rosemary

½ cup (18 g) dried lavender

½ cup (18 g) dried juniper berries

¼ cup (8 g) dried eucalyptus

¼ cup (8 g) dried mugwort

¼ cup (24 g) dried cedar

Mortar and pestle

3 star anise

Broom or vacuum

the ritual

In your large bowl, add in your salt. Three cups (876 g) is a general guideline; add or subtract based on the size of your home. Add your herbs one by one, focusing on your intention of protecting your home and removing any negative energies or spirits. Crumble the herbs between your fingers, working the herbs with your hands, infusing them with your energy. You can find eucalyptus or mugwort in "cut" form, so they are small bits; if you picked these yourself, crumble them in your hands as you drop them into the bowl.

In your mortar, grind the star anise into a powder. Sprinkle this into the bowl. Mix the salt and herbs together while chanting this incantation:

I call upon these
Herbs of protection
Banish all energies that wish to harm
Leave my home and heed this charm
Protect all who dwell in this home
No evil shall pass through the door
As this magic sweep protects this floor

Sprinkle this mixture all over your home. Let it sit for an hour, then sweep (or vacuum). If you are sweeping, make sure you sweep everything out the back door. You want this to exit your home, not welcome anything in. If you vacuumed, make sure you empty the canister or bag afterwards.

LEMON BALM SWEET DREAMS SLEEP SACHET

Nothing can be more troubling than nightmares. When you look forward to a good night's rest after a tough day, constant torture all night can leave you in a horrible mood when you wake up. Sometimes your entire day is ruined because you can't snap out of that mood and your mind is filled with those anxious thoughts from your dreams. There are rituals and charms from around the world to prevent nightmares, and I like this herbal blend best. This sleep sachet contains all the traditional relaxing herbs to get you to sleep, as well as ones that provide you protection during sleep. Lemon balm is a gentle, lemon-scented herb in the mint family that will help relax you and soothe you through the night.

ingredients
1 white candle
1 light blue candle
1 lavender candle
Hyssop Protection Oil (page 22) or a plant-based oil
1 tbsp (3 g) dried lavender
1 tbsp (3 g) dried rosemary
1 tbsp (2 g) dried mugwort
1 tbsp (2 g) dried rose petals
1 tbsp (2 g) dried chamomile
1 tbsp (2 g) dried lemon balm
Small lavender-colored bag
1 tumbled amethyst

the ritual

Do this ritual an hour or so before you go to bed. Choose smaller candles so they burn down before you fall asleep! Anoint them with oil, and take a few deep breaths.

Place your herbs one by one into your bag. Focus on feelings of relaxation, being well rested and free of any worries. Charge each herb as you place it into the pouch. Place the amethyst stone in the bag. Close your bag and place it in the center of the candles.

Say these words aloud:

Stars above
Light my way
Through the shadows
Of my dreams
Keep me safe until the dawn
Nothing can cause me harm
As I close my eyes to sleep
Bring me peace and serenity

Leave the pouch until the candles burn down. Take the sachet with you to bed and place it under your pillow. Feel relaxed, knowing that nothing can harm you as you sleep and that you will wake rested and happy.

ROSE EMPATH
SHIELD AMULET

Many of us who are drawn to witchcraft are empaths: some call it sensitive to energies, very intuitive, highly sensitive or clairsentient. You can easily feel the emotions of others and read their energy, but you are prone to take on other people's psychic gunk. You can have a heavy conversation with someone and feel exhausted, or even physically sick, after. People with emotional instability, narcissists, energy vampires (yes, that's a real thing) and people with issues tend to be drawn to us. Learn how to protect yourself so that you can avoid spending a lifetime with the weight of other people's problems on your shoulders. You need time to focus on yourself, and you cannot be an effective witch when you are bogged down. Learn to put up energetic boundaries to keep all of this junk at bay.

ingredients

Lavender incense

Vial pendant

Pinch of dried yarrow

Pinch of dried lavender

Pinch of dried rose petals

Pinch of dried cedar

Pinch of dried rosemary

Pinch of salt

Smoky quartz chips

Black tourmaline chips

16- to 24-inch (41- to 61-cm) length of chain or cord

Bowl

Sea salt

1 small white candle

the ritual

Take three deep breaths. Light your lavender incense. Pass your vial over the incense smoke to cleanse it. You can find these vials at craft stores, often already made with a loop on top to easily slide it onto a necklace.

Set your intention for protection. Begin to drop a pinch of each herb into the vial. Add in a pinch of salt, and the crystal chips. Place the cap on your vial.

Cut your length of chain or cord you want to use, and string the vial onto it. Place the finished amulet into a bowl of salt. Light your white candle and let it burn down while you focus on putting up boundaries against energy vampires. You are drawing a spiritual boundary around you to protect you. Once the candle has burned down you can wear this amulet.

ANGELICA CURSE PROTECTION CHARM

There will be times in your life when you have a friend, coworker, acquaintance or even a family member who doesn't have the best intentions for you. Perhaps they are envious of you or they are toxic, negative people. In extreme cases maybe they have cursed you or sent you some kind of negative intentions. This can also happen with a total stranger. Have you ever felt mysteriously ill or had a heavy pressure or headache after being out in public? Maybe you absorbed some negative energy from someone because you were totally open and defenseless to these extrasensory vibrations. Carry this charm with you always to feel protected from the evil eye, jealousy and negative intentions from others.

ingredients
1 red or black candle
Protective incense or a pinch of rosemary
1 tbsp (8 g) dried birch bark (if available)
1 tbsp (3 g) dried rosemary
1 tbsp (2 g) dried angelica
1 tbsp (6 g) dried lemon peel
1 tbsp (2 g) dried mint
1 tbsp (4 g) juniper berries
Pinch of black pepper
Pinch of chili pepper flakes or a single dried chili
Pinch of frankincense
Small black pouch
Black tourmaline or tumbled hematite

the ritual

This herbal charm is something that you can to carry with you to protect you. If you know who is sending you negative energies, you can keep it in your pocket or in your bag when you know you will see them. Or you can carry it for general protection, of course. If you live near a birch tree, collect a small twig or piece of its bark. Birch trees are very protective, and they are also considered purifying and cleansing to rid your aura of any negative energy.

You can inscribe your candle with protective words, phrases or even eyes. Light your candle. Light some protective incense or a pinch of rosemary. Now begin to place each herb into the pouch. Pass each herb through the incense invoking the energy of each herb to bring you protection. Place them in the pouch one by one. Lastly, add a black tourmaline or hematite stone. A shiny, energy-absorbing stone will reflect any evil eye away from you and back at the sender.

Once your pouch is complete, let the candle burn down. Focus on the protective properties of each herb and the shield of protection they will offer you.

PYRAMID PINE PROTECTION

Pine trees represent inner strength and overcoming adversity. They can be used for healing and for protection, which makes them a wonderful tree to use for this spell. Pyramids are renowned for their powerful, high vibrational energy. Use the strong, healing energies of the pyramid in the form of a candle. If you can't find a pyramid-shaped candle, you can form three candles into a triangle shape.

I created this ritual for the surgery of a close family member. It can be used to protect and provide strength to anyone undergoing a medical procedure, even pets. It helps put their mind at ease and protects them. You can also use this spell for any life-altering experiences, including going on a long trip or moving to a foreign country.

ingredients
Photo of a loved one
Pen
1 white pyramid-shaped candle or 3 white candles
Hyssop Protection Oil (page 22) or a plant-based oil
Pine Resin Protection Dust (page 28), divided
¼ cup (8 g) dried eucalyptus
¼ cup (12 g) dried lavender
¼ cup (8 g) dried sage
¼ cup (24 g) dried pine
¼ cup (13 g) dried rosemary
Small bowl

the ritual

First you will create a protection sigil (see page 161). Draw this sigil on the back of the photo. Place the photo on your table, and put the candle over it. Anoint your candle with oil. Sprinkle some protection dust on it.

Now you will create a protective barrier around your candle with the herbs. Take each herb in your hands and activate it for protection. Crumble them between your hands into a bowl. Add in a small amount of the protection dust. Mix all of the herbs together. Form a circle around the candle with the herb mixture.

Light your candle. Focus your energy on the candle. The center of healing is right above the photo. As the candle melts, the wax will envelop you or your loved one in a blanket of safety.

Say these words three times as the candle melts:

Pyramid of power
Keep (name) from any harm
Keep them safe and
Lovingly protected
Nothing shall cross
This barrier of herbs
Grant them strength
Grant them healing
They are protected
So mote it be

ST. JOHN'S WORT PSYCHIC ATTACK PROTECTION

Psychic attack is a form of negative energetic assault. This can happen consciously or unconsciously. You may have a toxic friendship, coworker or familial relationship where the other person holds these dark, venomous feelings for you. They might not consciously be cursing you, but they are projecting those energies onto you unintentionally. Carrying a protective amulet or sachet with you may be helpful, but it's also good to periodically do aura cleansings to shed all that toxicity.

This versatile recipe can be formulated to be done as a bath, a spray or an incense blend if you switch out a few ingredients. You can also use fresh herbs for this, if you prefer. Feet are especially vulnerable to absorbing unwanted energies, and St. John's wort has been used traditionally to ward off evil spirts and guard you from the evil. Vinegar is also commonly used for its protective and cleansing properties. Used in combination, they will clear your aura of any negativity.

ingredients
1 purple candle
Small basin or bucket
Water
½ cup (146 g) sea salt
½ cup (120 ml) apple cider vinegar
¼ cup (8 g) dried St. John's wort
¼ cup (13 g) dried rosemary
¼ cup (8 g) dried lemon balm
¼ cup (24 g) dried lemon peel

the ritual

Light your purple candle. If you have a separate basin for soaking, use that to waste less water and ingredients. You can do this in your bathtub if you need to. You can also light some incense or set the mood however you like before starting.

Fill your basin with warm water. Pour in your salt and vinegar. As you add each herb, call upon them to remove any negative energy and to cleanse you. Once you have everything in your basin, soak your feet for 20 minutes or so. You can close your eyes and meditate. Focus on your auric field and imagine a bright light coming through your head, moving all the way down your body to the soles of your feet. Feel your entire body pulsate with light.

After you are done, take the basin and pour it down your drain or into the earth. The earth helps transmute the energy and lets it dissipate. You can do this soak a few times a year to help clear away negative energy.

LOVE

Days: Friday and Monday
Moon Phase: full moon or waxing moon
Colors: pink and red

Love spells are some of the most ancient forms of magic, dating back to the ninth century. And for good reason. Who doesn't want love in their life? Love spells can be used for self-love, reuniting lovers or attracting a soulmate. It can get things going in the right direction with a current relationship, strengthen a marriage or open your heart up to new love. These spells can help open us up to seeing that love is all around us, even when we feel lost or alone. The first step to creating love magic is to know that you are worthy of having love and that you deserve it. It might be cliché, but it is true: you must learn to love yourself before you can love someone else.

It is important to note the concept of free will here. Love spells seem to be confused with the manipulation of another person. Now this all depends on who you ask. Some witches might not agree, and this might be controversial to some. You are NOT manipulating anyone to fall in love with you. You are simply creating your reality as you would like to see it. We aren't using "black magic," control or manipulation spells. This is lighthearted, fun and positive work. No person is being forced to fall in love with you. You can never deprive someone of their free will. You are creating the opportunity and the chance for your intention to manifest.

In this section, we will be using traditional herbs for love. What is the first herb that comes to mind when you think of love spells? Roses, of course. We will focus on rose, lavender, hibiscus, passionflower, rosemary, jasmine and bay leaf. Flowers with sensual, beautiful fragrance are important for drawing love to you. Have fun with these spells.

Rose is such a beautiful herb for love magic. They carry a watery, feminine energy that perfectly enhances spells for love. They have such a long history of magical use, from rosebuds and rosehips to petals and rosewater. All are symbolic of romance and love. For spells in this section we will focus mainly on red and pink shades, but you can use all colors on an altar depending on the intent.

Lavender is an herb that is beloved by so many. Its fragrance is used in everything from candles to soaps to impart the user with its relaxing, peaceful properties. Using lavender in sachets and in oils helps attract love through its fragrant flowers. Infusing paper with its scent can be good for writing love letters and spells.

Hibiscus is associated with lust, love and the planet Venus. It too carries a feminine energy in its deep red flowers. They can be used in tea, love sachets and incense to attract love. The hibiscus that is used for tea and in magic is an herb, unlike the big beautiful flowers that are reminiscent of tropical climates. Also known as roselle, these are small, garnet red, thick, fleshy calyxes. The calyxes are dried and cut for use.

Passionflower is a unique flower that looks almost otherworldly. It comes in a variety of colors from purple to white to red. The most commonly used passionflower is either purple or white. In herbalism it is used as a calming, sleep aid. It carries a feminine energy associated with the element of water and the planet Venus. This flower is said to bring back passion into a relationship, to ignite passion within yourself and to bring a passionate lover into your life.

Rosemary is a fiery, masculine herb. This can be used in conjunction with any of these other herbs to balance the more feminine, water element herbs. It can be used in love incense and sachets, to attract a lover. It is also commonly used in handfasting ceremonies or weddings to symbolize love and loyalty.

Jasmine is another classic flower associated with love. The fragrance alone is enchanting and alluring. It is ruled by the moon and all its divine feminine energy. It is said that it will attract a long-lasting, spiritually bound partner as opposed to strictly a physical connection. Use jasmine when you want to attract a soulmate.

Bay Leaf is used in many different ways. Love spells can call for a single leaf where you inscribe the names of the two lovers, or you can burn a bay leaf to make your wishes and desires come true. Bay can be placed on your altar or worn as part of a flower crown during love spells. It is said that lovers who want to stay together forever should break off a twig from a bay laurel tree and each will keep half.

HEART-OPENING
TEA RITUAL

Many times when we want to attract love, we come across roadblocks. We don't understand why relationships aren't working out or why love never seems to last. We often experience trauma in life, especially in childhood, that blocks us from what we truly want. We hold on to past negative experiences that keep us locked into unhealthy patterns and cycles. We need to open up our hearts to love. We need to unblock the heart chakra to truly receive love. Often this involves learning self-love and that all begins with us. This tea ritual should be done when we feel a blockage in our hearts. Whether you are single, in a relationship or just working on yourself, this is useful for all situations. I will give you two options for this tea, depending on whether you prefer an all-herbal tea or a caffeinated version. The herbal blend is also wonderful and light as an iced tea for those times of year when drinking hot tea is undesirable.

ingredients

Herbal Rose Tea

2 tbsp (4 g) rose petals
1 tbsp (4 g) hibiscus
1 tbsp (2 g) lemon balm
1 tsp lavender
1 tbsp (6 g) dried orange peel
Bowl

Cardamom Vanilla Tea

1 tbsp (2 g) black tea
(Darjeeling is my favorite)
1 tbsp (2 g) rose petals
4 cardamom pods
1 (1-inch [2.5-cm]) piece of vanilla bean
Small piece of cinnamon stick or
1 tsp cinnamon chips
1 tsp cacao nibs
Pinch of pink peppercorns
Bowl

the ritual

Drinking tea is as much of a ritual as other kinds of spell work. You want to put the same focus and intention into each ingredient. The measurements in these recipes should form a rough framework for your blends. Making tea blends is all instinctual. Blend however much of each herb you like. You can also make a larger batch of this tea to keep in your cupboard. If you plan on making a larger batch, do it as parts. For example, use 2 parts rose, 1 part hibiscus, 1 part lemon balm, ½ part lavender, 1 part orange peel.

Place each herb into a bowl one by one. Ask each herb to bring you love, self-love and healing of your heart. You can cup each herb in your hand, placing the other hand over it, blessing each herb. Once you have all your herbs in your bowl, mix it together, again focusing on healing of the heart.

Make your tea using 2 tablespoons (weight will vary) of herbs per cup (240 ml) of water. I always like to have a special mug or teacup that I use because it adds that extra touch of magic. If you are drinking out of a really beautiful teacup or glass, it makes the experience feel special.

Take three deep breaths. Imagine a soft pink healing light entering into your body every time you breathe in. Every time you breathe out, imagine letting go of any uncomfortable thoughts and sensations. Feel your body light, alive and vibrating with this healing energy. As you take each sip of tea, feel yourself surrounded with love. Give gratitude for everything you do have, and let go of anything you feel is lacking. When you give gratitude for what you have, you allow more space to bring in what you want.

Make this a daily routine. Take the 15 minutes out of your day to do this and soon you will find yourself overflowing with an abundance of love.

DRAWING LOVE
HIBISCUS BATH

There is nothing dreamier than a bath full of flower petals. This love bath includes all the beautiful flowers and herbs associated with love. It's meant to draw a lover nearer to you, but it can also be used for self-love. If you are looking to surround yourself with love and feel its vital energy, this is the perfect ritual. Perform this ritual on a Friday evening, preferably just before bedtime. When you visualize your perfect love you want to go to sleep right after to soak in all that positive energy. It is also best if you don't speak to anyone after the bath. Go to bed rested, knowing your love is being drawn closer to you. You can also do this bath before performing any other love rituals to get your mind in the right space for love.

ingredients
3 tbsp (6 g) dried hibiscus
3 tbsp (9 g) dried rose buds
3 tbsp (9 g) dried red rose petals
3 tbsp (9 g) dried lavender
3 tbsp (6 g) dried jasmine
Mortar and pestle
Muslin bag
Rose quartz
Splash of rosewater
Handful of fresh red rose petals
Handful of fresh pink rose petals
Pink candles

the ritual

Make sure your space is clean and tidy before beginning. Draw your bath. While your bath is filling, place all your dried herbs in your mortar. Grind the herbs to release the fragrance. Place all the herbs into a muslin bag. Let the bag soak in the water for a few minutes.

Place your rose quartz in the water. While you are preparing your bath, focus on the feeling of love and what you wish to draw into your life. Do not let your mind wander to anything else. Add the rosewater. Sprinkle the fresh rose petals across the top of your water.

Immerse yourself in the tub. Take a few deep breaths. As you feel more relaxed, begin to light your pink candles. Focus on your intentions. Imagine yourself in a beautiful, loving relationship. You can focus on the candle burning or close your eyes. Really soak up the feeling of love. Let yourself enjoy the bath for about 20 minutes.

ROSEMARY LOVERS
CANDLE SPELL

This spell should be done when you want to bring someone closer to you—a lover you have had a quarrel with or perhaps a crush that you wish to get closer to. It is especially effective for reuniting lovers. This spell is for a specific person, not to be used for love in general, and it will be done over the course of seven days. It calls for fresh rosemary and bay. These are relatively easy to find at a grocery store, but you may have them growing in your yard or already know where you might find them. Take a walk around your neighborhood; perhaps there is even some you can forage.

ingredients
Sewing pin

2 pink candles

Optional: Rose Come to Me Love Oil (page 62)

Handful of fresh rosemary sprigs

Handful of fresh bay leaves

the ritual

Using the pin, carve your name into one candle and your desired partner's name into the other candle. You can use rose oil to anoint the candles if you choose. Pour a small amount of oil onto each candle, and rub the oil all over the candle.

Place the candles about a foot (30 cm) apart. Create a circle around the two candles using the rosemary and bay leaves. Light your candles while focusing on bringing your love closer. Let the candles burn for about 10 minutes. Snuff, or pinch out the flame. You never want to blow the flame out.

On the second day you will move the candles a little closer together. Light the candles as the day before. Each day, you will move the candles closer to each other, until they touch on the seventh day. When the candles have burned out, the spell is done. Bury any remaining wax and the herbs in your yard.

HONEY ROSE LOVE RITUAL

This ritual was shared with me by a family member. Nearly everyone in my family has taken part in *limpias* or cleansings. When we get together our conversations often center around the occult, supernatural phenomena and our experiences going to curanderos. This ritual comes from a curandera in a small town near where my grandmother lives. It is for attracting love into your life. I have done this ritual, as have other friends and family members I have shared it with. It works, almost too well. You need to make sure you are specific when you set your intention: whether it's a specific person or it's a set of traits you want the person to have. You don't want to attract just anyone. You want to send the energy in the right direction! This spell is simple, and you need only two ingredients. Red roses will attract a passionate, romantic love, and the honey will have a person after you like a bee to a flower!

ingredients
1 cup (240 ml) raw honey
1 red rose

the ritual

As with most rituals, you want to first clean your physical body. For this ritual, you will be taking a shower or a bath, whatever you choose. Shower as you normally would. When you are done, turn off the water and stay in the shower. Begin to imagine your specific person or simply a new love entering into your life.

Pour the honey from the top of your head down to your toes. Cover every inch of your body while affectionately calling love to you. Rub the honey into your hair, across your shoulders, down your torso, your legs and even the soles of your feet. Do not leave any part of your body uncovered.

Once you are fully coated in honey, take the red rose petals and shower yourself with them. Imagine you are being showered with love, affection and romance. Your true love is now entering your life. Grab your handful of rose petals and raise your arm over your head, gently letting the petals fall across your body. All the while, remember to be focused and invite love into your life. Be open, and most importantly believe it to be true.

Once you have finished, rinse your body once more with water. Let any negative emotions or thoughts surrounding past relationships or ingrained patterns flow off your body and down the drain. After you are done make sure to throw the rose petals away. Do not leave them in your trashcan or inside your house. I prefer to throw them out into the yard or bury them. Let them go back into the earth. Once this is complete, let it go. This is important with any ritual, just know it is coming. You don't know when or how, but know that soon love will enter your life.

ROSE COME TO ME LOVE OIL

I love making oils because they are so versatile. You can use this to anoint candles, petition papers, tools and, of course, yourself. You can even use a splash in a love bath. The herbs in this oil are equal parts love and lust, for a balanced, well-rounded kind of love. When I make this oil, I like to find a beautiful, decorative jar. Use a pink-tinted glass, or even better, a heart-shaped bottle! You can often find these at craft stores or secondhand stores. Use this oil to attract romantic love. Dab on your heart chakra or on your third eye before a love spell. Dress your candles in this oil when doing any kind of love spell to increase its potency. There really is no limit to its uses!

ingredients
1 small pink candle

Rose incense

Small jar with a lid

Mortar and pestle

3 tbsp (6 g) dried pink rose petals

3 tbsp (9 g) dried lavender

3 tbsp (6 g) dried jasmine

3 tbsp (6 g) dried hibiscus

1 small cinnamon stick

2 dried rose buds

1 vanilla bean, cut in half

2 pieces of dried rose stem

Pinch of rose quartz gemstone chips or small tumbled stones

Pinch of garnet gemstone chips or small tumbled stones

½ cup (120 ml) sunflower or other plant-based oil

Optional: rose essential oil

the ritual

Light a small pink candle and the rose incense. Take your jar and cleanse it over the smoke of the incense. If you have a single leaf of sage or cedar you can also use that. Get the smoke all around the jar, including the inside.

In your mortar, add the rose petals and charge them by placing your hands over the mortar. Imagine a soft pink light emanating from your hands. Focus on the intent of what you will use this oil for. Place the rest of the herbs in the mortar and do the same. Begin to crush the herbs focusing solely on your intentions. They don't have to be powdered, just slightly broken down. Place them in your jar.

Add in the cinnamon stick and rose buds whole. The rose buds represent you and your intended love. Slice your vanilla bean vertically into two pieces. Place these in the jar. Carefully take a dried rose stem and cut it in half or into two pieces that will fit into your chosen jar. If you have flowers from your past love, this is even better!

Add in the gemstone chips. Fill the jar to the top with oil. I like to use oils such as sunflower or grapeseed because they don't have much of their own fragrance. If you really want to take this oil to the next level, you can add a few drops of rose essential oil. This can be quite pricey, but the scent is beyond beautiful.

Cover the jar and let this oil infuse with the natural fragrance of the herbs. Once your oil is done, say these words aloud:

Lovers herbs of lavender and rose
Vines of vanilla and bark of cinnamon
Bring me love, pure and true
Romance and passion may ignite anew
Love, love, love
Come to me from above

Leave this oil to infuse for a month before you use it.

STRAWBERRY
SOULMATE POWDER

If you are looking to settle down and find the love of your life, this is the spell for you. If you have been dating and not having any luck or are finally ready to find your life partner, this powder will help draw them into your life. This love powder will draw long-lasting, true love, not just a fling. Strawberry leaf is associated with the planet Venus which is the love planet. It helps you overcome any issues standing in the way of finding real love. Soulmates can come in many forms, and you can have more than one soulmate in a lifetime. This also includes finding your twin flame, or even a soulmate friendship. This powder can bring you everlasting love in this lifetime or a life-long friendship. This powder can be used in romantic love spells or in friendship spells.

ingredients

Optional: hawthorn twig

Mortar and pestle

3 tbsp (9 g) rose buds

3 tbsp (6 g) dried rose petals

3 tbsp (9 g) dried lavender

1 cinnamon stick

3 tbsp (21 g) frankincense

3 tbsp (21 g) sandalwood powder

3 tbsp (6 g) dried strawberry leaf

3 tbsp (6g) dried yarrow

3 tbsp (12 g) whole cloves

Small bowl

1 tsp vanilla powder or a few drops of vanilla extract

3 drops rose or lavender essential oil

Small jar

the ritual

If you happen to live near a hawthorn tree, break a small branch or large twig from the tree. Hawthorn is associated with the heart, marriage, love and finding romance.

Place each herb in your mortar one by one. In a clockwise direction, grind your herbs down to a powder or small pieces. Focus on the qualities of the partner you want. Feel the emotions of what it would be like to be with this person. Are you married? Are you living together? How happy does this make you feel? Really get into it and let your emotions go into this. Feeling intense emotions helps raise the energy and charges your powder with these intentions.

Once your herbs are pulverized, place each herb one by one in your bowl. Add the vanilla powder and essential oil to your powder mixture. Use the hawthorn twig to stir your herbs together. If you don't have this, don't worry, use a wooden spoon. Once everything is well combined, place your powder into a jar. Say these words over your finished powder:

True love shall find me
Our paths are soon to cross
Everlasting love so true
My one and only
Is on their way

Store this powder in the covered jar. You can use this powder to sprinkle on yourself before you go out or sprinkle it around your house. You can also add it to a charm bag or a jar spell, basically anything you want to amplify with love energy. Of course it can be used on its own; you don't need to mix it with anything for it to work.

ROSEBUD LOVE BOTTLE

Witch jars or bottles are a beautiful way to do spell work and to showcase herbs. Clear bottles allow you to see all the herbs and flowers swimming through the honey and rosewater in this spell. It's pure magic in a bottle. Rosebuds signify a new beginning to a relationship. Whether your intention is for a new blossoming relationship or a renewed love with someone from your past, rosebuds will give the energy needed to begin anew. This spell can be done to find a new love, reunite with an old flame or even strengthen an existing relationship. It's all about the intention you put into the spell. You can even write your desired partner's name on the birch bark or cinnamon stick if you want to do this on a specific person. Honey is wonderful for sweetening the heart of anyone who you wish to attract.

ingredients
Small bottle or jar
Protective herb
Tray
3 red tealight candles
3 dried rose buds
1 tbsp (2 g) dried rose petals
1 sprig of fresh rosemary
1 small cinnamon stick or 1 tsp cinnamon chips
1 tbsp (2 g) dried hibiscus
1 birch twig or bark
Splash of rosewater
Honey
1 pink chime candle
Optional: flower blend from Self-Love Flower Ritual (page 72)

the ritual

Choose a small bottle that you find visually appealing. Cleanse the bottle with smoke from any protective herb. You can even light a sprig of dried lavender which is also associated with love to energetically cleanse both the inside and outside of your bottle.

Place the bottle on the tray or on an empty space on your altar. Place the three red candles around your bottle. Add each herb one by one into your bottle. Focus your intention of receiving love as you place each herb into the bottle. Place the twig or bark into the bottle. Birch trees represent divine feminine energy, love and beauty. You can also use bark or a leaf if you don't have a twig. Add a splash of rosewater. If you can make your own, use that instead! Lastly, fill your bottle to the brim with honey. Cap your bottle.

Place the pink candle over your bottle. Secure the bottom of the candle to the lid by burning the bottom of the candle with a match, then firmly pressing it onto the lid. Light the candle. Surround your jar with love sprinkles (if using) or take some of the rose petals and rose buds and sprinkle them in a circle around your jar. Let the pink candle burn down over the lid, sealing it shut.

Place the jar on your altar, a shelf or any safe place. Love will soon enter your life.

CARDAMOM LOVE PERFUME

This perfume is to enhance lust and love. If you are in a relationship, it will spark the fire between you and enhance feelings of passion and love whenever you wear it. If you are single it will bring close your desires. Cardamom is a spicy, warming and sensual herb. It is highly stimulating for both the mind and body. It is considered to be one of the aphrodisiacs of the herb world. It brings a lusty, seductive energy to any love perfume or spell it is used in. Wear this perfume before you go on a date or for special occasions with your partner. Or wear it every day to enhance lust in your relationship.

ingredients
Love incense
1 tbsp (2 g) dried red rose petals
1 tbsp (2 g) dried pink rose petals
1 tsp dragon's blood
1 small piece of vanilla bean or vanilla extract
1 small cinnamon stick or 1 tsp cinnamon chips
1 tbsp (7 g) cardamom pods
1 tsp cloves
Small jar or bottle with a lid
Vodka
1 red chime candle

the ritual

Begin by lighting your incense. Choose whatever incense brings about feelings of love and passion. You can try cinnamon, rose, dragon's blood or cardamom. Play music in the background that makes you feel loved. Take your herbs one by one and charge them with your intentions and energy. Lightly crush the cardamom and cloves to release their scent.

Place the herbs in the jar one by one. Really focus your attention and energy during each step. When all the herbs are in your jar, top it off with vodka. Place the lid on your jar. Light the end of the candle to melt the wax and stick it on top of the lid. Let the candle burn down, sealing the jar with its passionate, loving energy.

Let the herbs infuse for 2 to 4 weeks before using the perfume. Wear this as you would any other perfume on your wrists, neck or right over your heart. You can leave the herbs in or strain them out.

LOVER RETURN
PASSIONFLOWER SPELL

Use this spell when you want a lover to return. Perhaps you feel as though the relationship can be repaired or that you still have a lot of love left with this person. This spell could not be any easier. All you need to find is fresh passionflower vine. Passionflowers bloom throughout summer, so late spring through the summer is when these are easiest to find. Try growing your own plant, or try finding some around your neighborhood. I once had a neighbor who had a plant that grew all along our fence—I was so grateful for it! Passionflower is said to reignite passion in a relationship, and when taken as a tea is very relaxing.

ingredients
Passionflower vine
Water
Teacup

the ritual

All you need for this ritual is a length of passionflower long enough to hang over your front door. It can be several pieces or one long piece, it doesn't matter. You can also hang it from your bedroom door. Make sure you use passionflower from your own garden or from a source that doesn't use pesticides. If it makes you feel more comfortable, you can buy passionflower tea and simply bury the fresh passionflower in your yard after the 3 days.

Drape the vine over your door. Leave it up for 3 days. On the third day, make a tea from the leaves. As you drink this tea, imagine your lover returning to you. They are on their way back to you. Know it in your heart that they will be back.

SELF-LOVE FLOWER RITUAL

This spell harnesses the uplifting, high vibrational energy of flowers. Flowers can be healing both physically and emotionally. This spell is fun, lighthearted and simple. This mixture of flowers is perfect for self-love and confidence. The energy of the flowers helps you emotionally heal and foster total, complete love for yourself. This, in turn, will attract all kinds of love into your life. All you need is a selection of flowers.

You don't need to use every single flower listed, but use as many as you can find. If you have a flower that you feel drawn to, then substitute it in this mix. After you complete the spell, use this flower blend to sprinkle over other love spells, to dress your candles with, as a bath or in a sachet. This enhances the energy of other spells. You can use fresh flowers if you have access to them, or use dried and keep them in a jar for later use.

ingredients

Mirror
1 pink candle
2 bowls
5 tbsp (10 g) dried red rose petals
5 tbsp (10 g) dried pink rose petals
5 tbsp (10 g) dried jasmine
5 tbsp (15 g) dried lavender
5 tbsp (10 g) dried hibiscus
5 tbsp (10 g) dried cornflower
5 tbsp (10 g) dried red clover

5 tbsp (10 g) dried calendula
5 tbsp (10 g) dried pansy
5 tbsp (10 g) dried violets
5 tbsp (10 g) dried chamomile
5 tbsp (10 g) dried orchid
5 tbsp (10 g) dried yarrow
5 tbsp (10 g) dried honeysuckle
Water
Jar for storage

the ritual

Do this spell on a Friday night, preferably on a full moon or waxing moon. Set up your mirror near a window so that it reflects the light of the moon. Light your pink candle and place it next to the mirror.

In a bowl, gently mix all your flowers together while focusing on the intention of self-love. You want to feel worthy and deserving of love—not only the love of others but of yourself. Inhale the beautiful fragrance as you imbue your energy into the flowers. Once your flowers are combined, sprinkle a handful into your second bowl. Add in lukewarm water. Let the flowers absorb some of the water. Watch them as they unfurl and swirl in the water. Continue to feel the love energy. You can compliment yourself as you look in the mirror. Tell yourself what it is that you love about yourself. After about 5 minutes, use this flower water to wash your face.

Take a few deep breaths and turn your gaze toward the mirror. See yourself as worthy and beautiful. You are capable, strong and perfect. Let these thoughts reflect upon the mirror as you continue to stare into your soul.

Say these words as you stare into yourself:

I am divine
I am heavenly
Exactly as I am
Abundance of love flows
Within me, without me
Within me love grows
And without love shows

Continue to gaze into the mirror as the candle burns down. Allow the moon's light to envelop you. Feel the deep love you feel for yourself. You will begin to attract love once you truly feel this love for yourself. Store the extra flowers in a jar for later use.

GINGER PASSION POTION

This potion is made to enhance the lust and passion in a relationship. It can be shared with a potential partner or used if you are already in love to increase the passion between you. It contains all the ancient herbs and spices that have been used to ignite romance and lust, along with the lusty fruits of cherry and strawberry. This is an adaptation of traditional wine love potions that have existed for centuries. Ginger and cardamom warm you up and act as mild aphrodisiacs, while rose petals keep the feelings of love flowing. You can drink this together on an evening in, or give it to your partner or crush to increase his or her passionate feelings for you.

ingredients
1 (1-inch [2.5-cm]) piece of fresh ginger
1 tbsp (7 g) cardamom pods
1 tbsp (2 g) dried red rose petals
1 tbsp (2 g) dried hibiscus
1 tbsp (6 g) fresh or dried orange peel
1 vanilla bean
1 cinnamon stick or 1 tbsp (8 g) cinnamon chips
5 cloves
5 fresh cherries
5 fresh strawberries
Decorative bottle
Squeeze of honey
1 bottle of red wine
Rose quartz
Garnet
Red jasper
Handful of fresh red rose petals

the ritual

This potion should be made 1 to 2 days ahead of time. You want all the magical love herbs to infuse into your wine. Charge each ingredient with passionate love energy as you drop each herb into the decorative bottle. After all the herbs and fruit have been added, squeeze a little honey into the bottle. The honey is symbolic for sweetening the other's feelings for you. It is not meant to make the wine sweet so don't add too much. Fill your decorative bottle with the entire bottle of wine. You can use any variety you like, making sure it isn't too acidic, too fruity or too sweet to ensure it doesn't clash with the herbs.

Place the stones around the bottle in a pyramid formation. Hold the rose petals in your hand and slowly shower the bottle while saying these words:

Love's delight, love's desire
Burn within us the passionate fire
May our lust grow
May our passion grow
May our love grow

Leave your potion to infuse with the herbs and stones for 1 to 2 nights. Once opened, the wine should be drunk promptly, as opened wine doesn't last long. Drink the potion over the course of 1 or 2 nights.

YARROW HANDFASTING OIL

Handfasting is the witch's version of marriage in many pagan traditions. It is symbolic, but not legally binding, so many people incorporate it into modern wedding ceremonies. It is a beautiful ritual that ties the couple's hands together with a cord to symbolize a spiritual union, with a promise of love for as long as love lasts. Whether a person chooses a more formal marriage or a handfasting, this oil can be used to give your partner a nudge in the right direction. This should be used if you are already in a relationship and wish to be married. It is also great for keeping faithful and strengthening an existing marriage or union. Yarrow is traditionally used in marriage and wedding rituals because it ensures love for at least seven years. Lemon verbena makes you appear beautiful and attractive to your partner always. Honeysuckle will keep you and your partner committed and in love forever.

ingredients

Small jar with a lid
3 tbsp (6 g) dried yarrow
2 tbsp (4 g) dried lemon verbena
2 tbsp (6 g) dried lavender
2 tbsp (4 g) dried rose petals
2 tbsp (4 g) dried honeysuckle
2 tbsp (4 g) dried jasmine
2 dried violets
2 dried rose buds

2 dried strawberry leaves
Optional: 1 Herkimer diamond
or clear quartz
1 dried bay leaf
Magical Love Ink (page 78) or a
pink or red marker
Sunflower or other plant-based oil
1 (24-inch [61-cm]) piece of pink thread
2 pink taper candles

the ritual

The act of creating magical mixtures sometimes requires you to do a little extra work to find your ingredients. It helps add energy when you find each ingredient whether on a walk, from a friend's garden or spontaneously somewhere unexpected. If you can find a strawberry leaf from a plant you saw on a walk or honeysuckle from a secret park, this adds to the energy of the spell. Pick a small amount to keep for future spells.

For this oil, cleanse whatever jar you will be using. Since this is for marriage you can use a beautiful pink or ornate jar but any glass jar will work. Charge each plant as you place it in the bottle. Focus on the intentions of marriage and a long-lasting union. This is optional, but since this oil is for an everlasting union, you can add a Herkimer diamond into your oil. This will represent the symbolic ring you want to receive. If you can't find Herkimer diamonds, you can use a faceted clear quartz or other stone you would like to see on your ring. The last herb you will add is your bay leaf. With your love ink, write the full name of your partner on one side and your name on the other. Place that in the jar. Once you have all the ingredients in the jar, add oil to the top.

Take your thread and bind the two candles together. Light your candles on top of or next to your jar. Let them burn all the way down.

As you watch the flame, say these words aloud. Chant them seven times, using emotion and strong energy:

Everlasting love come my way
Union and marriage are mine to stay
Keep my love alive and true
Forever bound to my one and only

Once your candle has burned down, store this oil, covered with a lid, in a safe place or on your altar. Now you can use this to dress candles, as an anointing oil or perfume—anything you want.

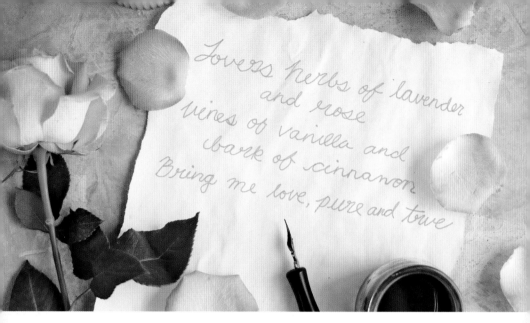

MAGICAL LOVE INK

This ink can be used to write spells in your book of shadows or to write anything as part of a love spell. If you need to write names or special sigils as part of a spell, use this ink to give them a little extra oomph. Dragon's blood aids in the potency of your spell work no matter the intention. Making magical inks requires a little experimentation—you might need to add a little more of this or a little more of that to get the right consistency. Once you learn to do this process, you can try substituting other powdered herbs or resins to create different colors and inks for other kinds of spell work. To use this ink, you will need a calligraphy pen or a quill.

ingredients
2 parts dragon's blood

Mortar and pestle

10 parts high-proof alcohol (Everclear, pure isopropyl alcohol)

1 tsp red wine or Ginger Passion Potion (page 74)

1 tsp rosewater

2–3 drops rose, lavender, ylang-ylang, patchouli,
neroli or jasmine essential oil

1 part gum arabic

Small jar with a lid

Red or pink rose petals

1 small red candle

To begin, you will need to first powder your dragon's blood. Take a small chunk of the resin, and place it in your mortar. Grind it until it reaches a fine powdered consistency. Add in your alcohol and mix it until it dissolves. You need a high-proof alcohol for the resin to really dissolve. If you use a regular vodka, the ink will work, but there will be a lot of sediment at the bottom.

For the wine, you can use 1 teaspoon of the Ginger Passion Potion, or use whatever wine you have on hand. I like to use the last leftover sip from a wine glass, since it is imbued with all your energy. You can take the wine in your mouth and spit it into the bottle, or simply pour it in. Taking it in your mouth lets your energy really meld with the wine. There is a part of you within the ink that empowers it even more.

Add in 1 teaspoon of rosewater. You can add 2 to 3 drops of any essential oil that is symbolic of love. Lastly, mix in 1 part gum arabic. This acts as a thickening agent and allows the ink to really stick to your pen so that the ink flows smoothly. This will take some trial and error. If you need more gum arabic, add it in small increments until your ink has reached the right consistency.

Pour your finished ink into a small, shallow jar that you can easily dip your pen into. Place the jar on your altar or a space where it will remain undisturbed overnight. Sprinkle your jar with red rose petals. Take a small red candle, and melt the bottom and place it onto the lid of the jar. Light the candle and let it burn down to charge your ink. Once the candle has burned down, leave the jar there overnight and it is ready to use.

ABUNDANCE

Days: Sunday and Thursday
Moon Phase: full moon, new moon or waning moon
Colors: green, yellow and gold

Abundance, prosperity, money . . . whatever you want to call it, we all need it to survive. Whether you want to boost sales in your business, pay off debt or find your dream job, you can use magic to manifest abundance in your life. We will use oils, powders, sachets and all different kinds of spell work to achieve your goals.

There are many herbs that are used for prosperity, but the ones that are most commonly used are cinnamon, basil, clove, nutmeg, chamomile, orange and ginger. These are all herbs and spices that are easy to find at a grocery store or that you can grow yourself. Many of you will already have these herbs in your kitchen cabinet! All of these herbs are associated with the sun and the element of fire. This really speaks to the power of these herbs to work for your ritual!

When doing spells for abundance, remember you must give in order to receive. Doing money spell work is not about being greedy and not doing anything in return. Always be grateful. Give thanks for anything that comes your way and give it back to others, and it will keep on coming back to you. Whether this means generously tipping at a restaurant, giving friends gifts for no reason or paying for your little brother's birthday party. Do this out of good will, without expecting or feeling deserving of anything. Once you have learned how to do this, money will never be lacking.

Cinnamon is probably the number 1 herb that is used in money spells. In herbalism, cinnamon is a warming herb that increases circulation. Energetically, cinnamon is fiery, fast-moving and brings in the energy of the sun. In magic rituals, cinnamon helps speed up the energy and brings your desire fast. It holds a high vibration, making it ideal to work with in spell work.

Basil is not only a fantastic-smelling herb with culinary value, it's also used to attract money. Like cinnamon, basil also has a fiery, masculine energy. A single leaf can be kept in your wallet, cash register or purse to bring in abundance. A water made with basil can be sprayed in your business, place of work or on your doorstep to protect your money or bring in more money.

Cloves are similar to cinnamon, in a magical sense. They are also a fiery, intensely scented spice. We most often think of cloves as being used in baking, for making mulled wine and as a winter solstice herb. Cloves work well in combination with cinnamon as they work together to intensify the energy of the spell. Cloves are used in abundance spells as well as spells for luck.

Nutmeg is associated with the element of air. It can be used in its whole or powdered form. Use it in money-drawing oils or powders to draw in abundance. Nutmeg is ruled by Jupiter, the planet of luck and prosperity. Carrying a whole nutmeg, or stringing it onto a necklace, is said to bring the wearer good luck and fortune. Keeping a nutmeg with you works as a type of amulet or charm.

Chamomile is one of my favorite herbs. It is used as mild nervine to soothe the mind, diminish anxiety and reduce stress. I use it all the time in medicinal preparations, but it is also a great herb to attract abundance. Chamomile was considered a sacred herb in ancient Egypt, and was dedicated to Ra, the sun god. Like basil, you can carry a pressed chamomile flower in your wallet or purse to attract money. Chamomile, like most of the herbs on this list, is associated with the sun. Do you see a pattern arising here? Fast-moving, high-energy sun herbs bring in the prosperity!

Orange, like most citrus, is an uplifting, happy energy. Yes, this too is a sun energy herb. Technically orange is a fruit, but you can use the peel in herbal formulations. I think oranges are an underrated element in spells. Most of us think of using herbs, or spices, but fruit and flowers are also important in spell work. Oranges, whether used fresh or in dried form, aid in bringing in abundance and prosperity.

Ginger, the last herb we will cover, is considered both food and medicine. Ginger is a hot, spicy, fast-acting herb. It can be used as a fresh root, dried slices or powdered. You can even keep the plant in your garden to bring in abundance. One of my favorite ways to use ginger is as a tea to soothe indigestion. If you want to add an extra zing to your spell, try drinking a ginger tea before your grounding process to help protect your spell and aid it in working with speed. Adding ginger to your food can create a magical experience. Ginger will act as a catalyst in energizing your spells, so get ready to receive your manifestation quickly when you add ginger!

BASIL MINT
ABUNDANCE BATH

Spraying basil water around your home is a well-known money drawing ritual. Bathing in basil is also meant to draw in abundance. Keep in mind that abundance can mean much more than financial security. Abundance can be happiness, feeling good, a general sense of well-being and a zest for life. Spirulina adds the energy of the color green. Color therapy can be used for many purposes within magic, including for prosperity and good fortune symbolized here by the color green. Green also represents balance and harmony. When you want to attract abundance, make sure you have a balance of giving as well. To receive, you must give freely and with love—not with expectation. Use this bath if you want to attract money and for any form of abundance you desire.

ingredients
Green or gold candles
Optional: aventurine, citrine or pyrite crystals
Handful of fresh basil or ¼ cup (18 g) dried basil
Handful of fresh mint or ¼ cup (8 g) dried mint
Handful of fresh chamomile or ½ cup (14 g) dried chamomile
5 sliced oranges or ¼ cup (24 g) dried orange peel
Muslin bag
1 tbsp (10 g) spirulina powder
1 cinnamon stick

the ritual

For this bath you can use either fresh or dried herbs. If you are using fresh herbs, you can float them in the water, but the dried version should be placed in a muslin bag or made into a tea beforehand. I like to use fresh herbs when I can, and mint and basil are easily found in any grocery store if you prefer to use fresh. I have found fresh chamomile many times at farmers' markets or ethnic grocery stores.

Make sure your bathing area is clean and free of mess. Light your candles. Place them around your tub or on a bath tray if you have one. If you are using crystals, place them in the water or around the edge of the tub.

Charge each herb by focusing on your intention of bringing in abundance and prosperity. Place your herbs one by one into a muslin bag. Include the dried orange peel, if using. Once all your herbs are in the bag, let it steep in the bathwater for a few minutes. Alternatively, if you prefer you can make a tea from the herbs and pour it into your bathwater.

Add in the spirulina powder. Light the cinnamon stick, and use it as incense. Waft the smoke all around your bath area. Cinnamon activates other herbs and speeds your work along. If you are using fresh orange slices, instead of dried, float them on the water.

Take a few deep breaths and step into your bath. Let any worry or stress about your situation go. Focus on what you need this money for. How will you use it? Imagine yourself with your wallet or bag full of money to pay for whatever you need. You are abundant and without any worry. Soak in the bath for 20 to 30 minutes. Anytime your mind wanders to feeling a lack of abundance, don't get frustrated; just watch the thought flow out of your mind and down the drain, away from you.

You can do this bath on its own or before performing some abundance spell work. Keep positive, focus on attracting prosperity and it will begin to flow into you.

CINNAMON PROSPERITY INCENSE

Making incense is a great way to get prosperity flowing into your life. This can be used in conjunction with spell work or on its own. Unlike a specific spell, you can burn this daily if you want to enhance the energy of prosperity in your home. You will break up whole herbs with your mortar and pestle; powdered herbs aren't recommended, but use them if that's all you have. All of these herbs are great for bringing in abundance, but cinnamon and ginger really speed things up if you are under a time crunch. Try to make this incense on a new moon, but make it on any day if you are in a time of need.

ingredients
3 tbsp (12 g) whole cloves
3 tbsp (18 g) allspice
Mortar and pestle
4–5 cinnamon sticks or ¼ cup (32 g) cinnamon chips
3 tbsp (16 g) dried ginger
3 tbsp (6 g) dried mint
3 tbsp (14 g) dried basil
3 tbsp (18 g) copal
Small jar

the ritual

Place your cloves and allspice in your mortar. I like to put herbs that have a similar consistency in together: the harder, woodier herbs together and the herbaceous leaves together. With each herb, place your hands over it as you infuse the intention of receiving money into each one. Grind the herbs in a clockwise direction, bringing abundance toward you.

Break up the cinnamon sticks into smaller pieces and grind them with the cloves and allspice. You don't need to create a powder, just break them down into small pieces. Next add your ginger, mint and basil.

Once you have prepared the herbs, add in your copal. Continue to mix them together with your hands. Make sure to focus on the intention of generating more money and bringing in prosperity. Focus on it coming to you quickly.

Store your finished incense in a jar. To use it, burn a small pinch on a charcoal disc. Waft the smoke on any candles or other tools you will be using, or burn it on its own! As you burn this incense throughout your home, business, room or altar space you can say these words:

Money money come to me
Abundance comes to me I decree
Fill my pockets, fill my hands
Overflow with coins
So shall I have

ABUNDANCE HERBAL AMULET

Amulets have long been used for protection, healing and bringing good luck and prosperity. They are also called mojo bags, spell bags or charm bags. Amulets can be used for almost any specific purpose you have. This amulet will draw abundance into your life. Use it to create more sales in your business, attract money during difficult times or simply bring more wealth into your life. You will be using herbs long associated with abundance and prosperity. I also chose three crystals that are well known for drawing in abundance.

This ritual calls for making your own green amulet out of fabric. My belief is the more intention and the more you work a spell, the more energy it creates, which is why I choose to sew my own amulet. The more your hands work the tools, the stronger the energy that is put into it. If you already have a small fabric bag, you can substitute it.

ingredients

2 pieces of green felt or green flannel fabric

Sewing needle

1 (16-inch [41-cm]) piece of green or gold thread

1 tbsp (5 g) dried basil

1 tbsp (4 g) whole cloves

1 small cinnamon stick or 1 tbsp (8 g) cinnamon chips

1 tbsp (7 g) frankincense

Pinch of pyrite chips

Pinch of citrine chips

Pinch of aventurine chips

4 coins (any currency)

1 gold candle

1 silver candle

1 green candle

the ritual

Set up all your supplies on your altar or designated space for doing ritual work. For me it's always important to have a dedicated space for doing magic in my home. If you like to work outdoors, set up a blanket or clean off an area where you can sit and do your ritual. Cut out two 3-inch (7.5-cm) squares from your green fabric. Felt is easy to find anywhere, but flannel is traditionally used in mojo bags. Any green fabric will work, but having a thicker fabric makes it easier to sew.

Take a few deep breaths, ground yourself and set your intentions for this ritual. Thread your needle with the thread, fold it in half and knot the ends. Place the two squares of fabric together and sew around the edges. Leave about ¼ inch (6 mm) around the edge. If you are using a fabric other than felt, make sure you place the two squares with the right sides of the fabric together. Once you turn it inside out the right sides will end up on the outside. Continue sewing until you have about a 1-inch (2.5-cm) piece left. Leave this open. This is where you will fill the pouch.

Place all your herbs, crystal chips and coins into the pouch. If your cinnamon stick is too large, break it into smaller pieces and drop them into the pouch. Fold in the edges of the open pouch and sew it shut. Once you are done sewing, tie off the end of the thread and cut any excess thread.

Place your amulet on your altar or on your sacred space outside. Light the three candles in a circle around your amulet. As they burn, chant these words:

Herbs and coins work your magic
With the aid of these ancient stones
Abundance and prosperity shall I own
As I work this sacred rite
My fortune will increase tonight
Money come to me from near and far
With the power of my lucky star

Once you are done with the chant, keep this pouch on your altar. You can also keep it in your place of business, on your work desk, in your purse or in your pocket. Keep it where you want the money to flow.

ROSEMARY PROSPERITY
SWAG

This herbal swag is made to adorn your front door to attract prosperity like a magnet. Unlike most of the rituals in this book, this swag requires that you use all fresh herbs. The herbs need to be pliable so that you can bundle them together without them crumbling. If you have access to only a small amount of fresh herb, make a smaller bundle to hang on your doorknob or place in the entryway. Your front door is the portal to your home, so placing these abundance-attracting herbs at the door invites prosperity and good fortune to flow to you. You are welcoming positivity to pass through your door.

ingredients
10–15 sprigs of fresh rosemary
10–15 sprigs of fresh common sage, pineapple sage or black sage
10–15 sprigs of fresh mint
A few handfuls of bay leaves
1–2 cinnamon sticks
Gold string or wire
Optional: gold ribbon

the ritual

Lay out all your herbs on your workspace and set your intention. Imagine the money you need flowing into your home. Imagine a check you've been waiting for, a surprise tax refund or however you imagine money entering your life. Charge the herbs with your hands, and empower them for the use of obtaining money.

An herbal or floral swag is basically a large herbal wand that is wrapped only on one end. If you don't have a lot of fresh herbs, this allows you to still create something you can hang without having to make a full wreath. Use 10 to 15 sprigs of each herb—or more depending on how lush you want it to appear.

To begin making the swag, gather your herbs into a small bundle, layering the smaller leaved herbs on top of the larger ones. Add the cinnamon to the base, or stem end of the swag. Tie it together with gold string or wire. If you want to add a gold ribbon, tie that to the swag.

Hang the herbs on your door to attract prosperity to your home.

PYRAMID PROSPERITY CLOVE SPELL

Cloves are associated with the planet Jupiter, and they carry the energy of the element of fire. This makes them extremely potent. Cloves can be used for a variety of spell work, but using them for prosperity spells brings you good luck and wealth quickly! Pyramid shapes also contain a potent energy within them. This is why the ancient Egyptians chose this powerful form for their great pyramids. Working with the pyramid shape generates a sort of vortex that allows you to generate and amplify energy in order to draw in prosperity. You can also use pyramid-shaped candles or crystals to mirror this same energy. Do this spell when you want to work on building long-term prosperity. This is not a get-rich-quick scheme, but a way for you to remain prosperous.

ingredients
Mortar and pestle
5 tbsp (20 g) whole cloves
5 cinnamon sticks or 5 tbsp (40 g) cinnamon chips
5 tbsp (23 g) dried basil
4 pyrite stones, divided
Paper
Green or gold pen
Metal tray or plate
$20 bill (or any denomination)
1 magnet
3 gold candles
Green string

the ritual

In your mortar, crush your cloves, cinnamon and basil. Place each herb in one at a time focusing on bringing in prosperity and abundance. You can chant these words aloud: "Money, abundance, prosperity, come to me!" Continue to say these words as you work the spell. Set these herbs off to the side.

In your mortar, crush one of the pyrite stones into a powder. You can also find it already in powder form in some crystal shops. Mix the pyrite together with your herbs and set it aside.

On the piece of paper, draw an infinity sign with either gold or green pen. Place the paper on your tray, then place the $20 bill on top. Then place the magnet on top of both. Place your 3 gold candles in a pyramid formation around them. Sprinkle the ground herb and pyrite mixture in a circle around the candles. Place your 3 remaining pyrite stones next to each candle. Light your candles. Focus on your intention of bringing prosperity. Let the candles burn down. Dispose of the wax remains (page 183). Place the paper, the magnet and a pinch of the herb mixture inside the bill. Fold the bill toward you, three times. Wrap a length of green string around the packet to keep it closed. Make sure to wrap toward you, as if the money is flowing toward you. Carry this bundle in your wallet so that it should always be full.

MONEY FLOW CITRUS OIL

This oil, like all the others in this book, is versatile. You can anoint all your abundance candles, rub it on your hands, pour it into a sachet, rub it on a paper petition or add a splash to a bath. It uses high vibrational, fast-acting herbs that will allow any of your money spells to work quickly. Citrus fruits are also cleansing, so if you have any negative attachments with money or you are using this to cleanse debt, it works well for these kinds of issues. If you have a pile of bills stacking up that you are dreading, you can rub this on your hands before you get started. Anything relating to prosperity or abundance can benefit from having this oil as part of the spell.

ingredients
Cinnamon Prosperity Incense (page 86)
Small decorative jar with a lid
1 tbsp (6 g) dried lemon peel
1 tbsp (6 g) dried orange peel
1 tbsp (7 g) frankincense
1 tbsp (4 g) whole cloves
1 tbsp (6 g) allspice
1 tbsp (7 g) sandalwood powder
1 cinnamon stick or 1 tbsp (8 g) cinnamon chips
1 bay leaf
Optional: tumbled aventurine, pyrite, citrine or green agate
½ cup (120 ml) sunflower or other plant-based oil
1 green candle

the ritual

Light your incense. This sets the atmosphere for making the oil. Pick a small decorative jar that you find appealing for this ritual; it can even be green to represent money. As you take each herb in your hand, charge it with the intention of money flowing into your life. Place each herb in this way one by one into the jar. If you are using a crystal, add that in.

Fill the jar to the top with an unscented or lightly scented oil. Once your jar is full, set it on your altar. Light the bottom of your candle to melt the wax and firmly stick it on the top of your jar. Light the candle and let it burn down to charge the oil. Leave the jar for a month before using the oil.

ORANGE PEEL
FIND A JOB SPELL

This simple spell is for finding a job. Perhaps you are out of work or you are seeking a new or different job. Orange peel is said to attract good fortune and abundance. It also is representative of joy and happiness; this makes it a good herb for spells that will bring you work you enjoy. You will use three herbs and three candles to represent the job, paper money and coins. This spell will encourage employers to hire you or give you the nudge to find the right job. Of course, you must also do some work: continue to look for jobs, go on interviews and have a positive mind-set. Once you have the job, you will have all the money to pay your bills, have money to spend and will feel stable and grounded. No more anxieties surrounding lack of money. The perfect job for you is just around the corner!

ingredients
1 small brown candle
1 small yellow or gold candle
1 small green candle
Money Flow Citrus Oil (page 94) or a plant-based oil
Dried basil
Cinnamon powder
Dried orange peels
Optional: mortar and pestle
Tray or plate
Fresh basil leaf
Cinnamon stick
Orange slice

the ritual

For this spell, the brown candle will represent the job, having stability and being grounded knowing you have a source of income. The yellow or gold candle represents coins and the green candle represents paper currency. You will be attracting both to you, along with the job.

To begin, carve "money flows to me" into the green and yellow candles. Carve "I have my perfect job" into the brown candle. Dress your candles with the oil.

Roll your candle in the corresponding herbs: dried basil on the green candle; cinnamon on the brown candle; orange peels on the yellow candle. You can crush the orange peel in your mortar until they are fine so they will stick to the candle.

Focus on the settled, relaxed feeling you will have knowing your job is secure and you no longer need to worry about feeling lack. You are rolling in the money as you roll the candle in the herbs.

Arrange your candles on your tray with the brown candle in the center and the others on either side. Place your green candle over your fresh basil leaf. Break the cinnamon stick apart with your fingers and place it around the brown candle. Place the yellow candle in the center of your orange slice.

Light your candles, and say these words aloud:

Success, money and opportunity
All these three things flow to me
Bills and coins
Line my pockets
As I feel
The perfect job for me
Is on its way
So mote it be!

LEMONGRASS MONEY ROAD OPENER

You might feel stuck, like nothing is changing. Maybe you even feel like your other money spells aren't working. Or maybe you have lost your job or had a run of bad luck. Sometimes you need to do a spell to remove obstacles from your path in order for your spell to work faster—or to work at all. Lemongrass clears anything blocking your desires from manifesting, and it brings good luck. This spell can work for money spells or for success and luck spells. It's a good all-around spell to use when you feel stagnant in some way. This spell uses many of the same herbs used for abundance spells; you can easily incorporate any of the oils, powders or incense used in the previous rituals.

ingredients

1 large yellow candle

3 green candles

3 gold candles

Money Flow Citrus Oil (page 94) or a plant-based oil

Tray or plate

¼ cup (20 g) dried lemongrass

¼ cup (8 g) dried lemon balm

¼ cup (18 g) dried basil

¼ cup (24 g) dried orange peel

1 tbsp (6 g) allspice

1 tbsp (4 g) whole cloves

1 tbsp (8 g) ground cinnamon

7 star anise

3–5 cinnamon sticks

the ritual

To begin, dress your candles with your oil. Rub the oil down the candle, facing you. You are pulling the abundance toward you. Place them on your tray. Set the yellow candle in the center with the green and gold candles in a circle around it.

Focus your energy on each herb. Take it in your hand and enchant it with your intention. Sprinkle each herb around the candles. Once you have all the herbs on your tray, light your candles.

You want to break down anything standing in your path. Say these words aloud in a firm, demanding tone:

Break all barriers
Open all roads
Let abundance flow to me
Easily and freely
I have money in a constant flow
Quickly and easily
Because I do deserve
All things good
That come my way

Let the candles burn down. Since this might take several hours, you can place the tray in a bathtub, shower, sink or anywhere that you can be sure they won't catch fire. If you feel more comfortable, you can pinch the flame out and do this spell over a series of days until the last candle is burned. Once this spell is done, wait a couple of weeks before attempting to do more money spells.

TEA LEAF BUSINESS
SUCCESS SPELL

This spell is unique. Unlike most spells that you just let go out into the universe, this one requires you to constantly work with it. You need to give this spell attention. If you've started a new business or are in a financial slump, give this spell a try to help money quickly begin to flow into your bank account. Put this on your altar, your kitchen countertop or your dresser—anywhere where you will constantly see it. Whenever you have extra change or an extra dollar, you can add it to this spell to keep the energy flowing. Black tea is said to guarantee wealth and riches for the present and for the future. So this spell will guarantee your business will bring you lots of future financial success.

ingredients
Cinnamon Prosperity Incense (page 86)
Small gold- or green-colored bowl, jar, plate or cup
1–3 paper bills (any denomination)
Handful of coins (any denomination or currency)
3 cinnamon sticks
3 pinches of dried basil
3 pinches of dried orange peel
3 pinches of dried peppermint
3 pinches of black tea
Small scrap of paper
Gold or green pen
1 gold candle
Money Flow Citrus Oil (page 94) or a plant-based oil

the ritual

Light your incense and cleanse your bowl in the smoke. This is especially important if it's a bowl you have used for previous ritual work. I suggest you choose something new, but use what you have—I just wouldn't use it to eat out of again.

Begin by placing your paper bills in the bottom of your bowl. Then place the coins on top. You can use magical numbers to count out the number of coins you add or add a handful—it's up to you. You can also choose to add foreign currency if you want your business to attract money from all around the world.

As you place each herb into the bowl enchant it with your intention to bring in a constant flow of money. Close your eyes and hold each herb between your palms, and then place it in your bowl.

On a small piece of paper write your intention for this spell with gold or green pen. You can write something like Money Flow or even dollar signs. Whatever feels right to you. Fold the paper three times, each time folding the paper toward you, turning it to the right and folding it back toward you. When you fold the paper toward you, you invite the money to come to you. Place the paper in the bowl.

Carve your intentions into your candle. You can write the same thing you did on your paper or carve symbols that correspond to money. Dress your candle with the money oil. Place the candle in the bowl on top of the herbs on a small candle holder or next to the bowl. Light the candle and let it burn down.

Keep this bowl somewhere you will constantly see it. Every once in a while you can add some coins, a dollar bill or some fresh herbs. You can whisper to it "money flow, money flow"—anything that gives this bowl energy and will keep money coming to you!

BASIL BRING ME RICHES POWDER

This powder can be used in so many different ways: Sprinkle it on yourself, your doorstep or around your home. Use it in conjunction with other spells, for dressing candles or even making sigils on your altar. Its uses are endless. Some of the herbs in this recipe can be purchased already ground. If you want to buy them that's okay, but grinding them in your mortar really lets you infuse them with your energy. Comfrey can be found in most herbal supply shops. If you have trouble finding it, you can grow comfrey yourself or substitute herbs you feel called to use. It is said that you can wrap your money in a leaf of comfrey to keep it coming back to you.

ingredients

1 gold candle
Money Flow Citrus Oil (page 94) or
a plant-based oil
Cauldron or heatproof dish with sand
Charcoal
Basil or Cinnamon Prosperity Incense (page 86)
Mortar and pestle
7 cinnamon sticks or 7 tbsp (56 g)
cinnamon chips
7 whole nutmegs or 3 tbsp (21 g)
ground nutmeg

7 tbsp (42 g) allspice
3 tbsp (12 g) whole cloves
7 tbsp (42 g) dried orange peel
7 tbsp (28 g) dried comfrey
7 tbsp (35 g) dried basil
Pinch of pyrite chips
Bowl
Small glass jar or bottle
1 penny
1 nickel
1 dime
1 quarter

the ritual

Take your candle and rub it with oil. Carve your intentions for your powder into your candle. You can use words such as success, draw money, receive a raise, $$$, a specific amount of money or anything relating to your spell. Light your candle.

In your cauldron or heatproof dish with sand, light your charcoal. Put a pinch of basil or incense on top.

Add each herb one by one to your mortar. Break the cinnamon sticks into small pieces. I like to do all the harder, woodier herbs first. Once you have the cinnamon, nutmeg, allspice, cloves and orange peel done, you can either crumble the remaining herbs with your hands or grind them in the mortar. You can also powder your pyrite crystals this way, or you can often find them already ground in crystal shops.

Place all the powdered herbs and pyrite into a bowl. You can mix them with your hands or a spoon while you focus on drawing money to you. Add the powder to your jar. Add your coins to the jar.

Pass the jar through the smoke of the incense. Let the candle burn down and your powder is ready to use. Every time you shake the jar and hear the coins rattle, you are bringing the money toward you.

STRAWBERRY
SUCCESS CHARM

Abundance spells aren't just about receiving quick cash or an unlimited supply of money. Many times we are stuck in a job, we don't seem to be moving in any one direction and we want the universe to present us with opportunities. Maybe you have always wanted to start your own business and you are looking for investors or partners. Or maybe you want a raise, a new position, the chance to travel more or even explore a new career path. This ritual is perfect for attracting all kinds of positive changes into your life. If you are at a crossroads, try this ritual to open yourself up to accepting new, exciting opportunities. While it is not something that immediately comes to mind for magic, strawberry leaves have been used for centuries for luck spells. They can bring good fortune and attract success, while helping clear away stagnant patterns to make room for new endeavors.

ingredients
1 tbsp (2 g) dried chamomile

Charcoal disc

Large vial

3 strawberry leaves

1 tbsp (2 g) dried jasmine

1 tbsp (2 g) dried honeysuckle

3 dried red clover blossoms

1 star anise

the ritual

This charm can be kept on your desk at work, on your money altar, by your bed or anywhere you will see it on a daily basis.

Light a pinch of your chamomile on your charcoal disc. Pass your vial over the smoke to cleanse it.

Pass each herb through the same smoke. Focus on what new things you want to bring forth into your life: How amazing are you going to feel once you have broken free of your old, unfulfilling job. The freedom to do what truly feels satisfying and to make money at it.

As you set your intentions into each herb, place them in the vial. Once all the herbs are inside, cap the vial. If you want, you can charge this further with a candle or a crystal or leave it overnight under the moon. Anytime it catches your eye, remember, good things are coming.

COMFREY MONEY JAR

This spell works with the energy of Jupiter. Planetary energy is something that is used a lot by ceremonial magicians and other occult practices, but also by most witches. Jupiter is the planet of all abundance, wealth and good fortune. Comfrey is also ruled by the planet Jupiter. It can be used to attract abundance of all kinds. So for this ritual, you will be incorporating symbols of Jupiter. You can also incorporate your own money sigils to increase the power. If you want to learn more about making sigils, check out page 161.

ingredients

Cinnamon, mint, clove or patchouli incense

Small scrap of paper

Green marker

Money Flow Citrus Oil (page 94) or a plant-based oil

Small jar with a lid

3 tbsp (12 g) dried comfrey

3 tbsp (18 g) allspice

3 tbsp (6 g) dried chamomile

3 tbsp (12 g) whole cloves

3 tbsp (21 g) nutmeg

3 tbsp (6 g) dried mint

3 tbsp (6 g) dried patchouli

1 pyrite stone

1 small green candle

the ritual

Light your incense. On your scrap of paper, draw the symbol for Jupiter with green marker. If you are using your own money sigil, draw it here as well. Focus on the energy of drawing money to you. Pass the paper through the incense smoke, dab it with money oil or enchant it however feels right to you. Cleanse the jar with smoke and add in your Jupiter symbol.

Enchant each herb with your desire to draw money. Add them one by one to the jar. Add in your pyrite stone. Close the lid. Place your green candle over the jar and let it burn down.

Place your jar on your altar, or somewhere you will see it often. Shake the jar and continue to add your intentions every time you notice it. Money will begin to flow to you.

PUMPKIN PROSPERITY SPELL

Pumpkins are a symbol of prosperity. They can become an empty vessel for you to fill with herbs that will bring you abundance. The empty void within the pumpkin represents the unlimited potential for abundance. The seeds are also symbolic of fresh, new energy ready to be birthed. Rice is also symbolic of money across many cultures, and it is often used to represent success, wealth, luck and abundance in all forms. This is a great spell to do around Samhain— the halfway mark between autumn equinox and winter solstice—but you can do it all year long. If you can't find pumpkins or they aren't in season, you can substitute any type of squash, you can even use a watermelon.

ingredients
1 small pumpkin or any kind of squash
Money Flow Citrus Oil (page 94) or a plant-based oil, divided
1 cup (240 ml) honey
1 tbsp (8 g) ground cinnamon
3 tbsp (14 g) dried basil
3 tbsp (6 g) dried peppermint
3 tbsp (6 g) chamomile
1 tbsp (7 g) frankincense
3 cloves
Handful of rice
Splash of mint water
1 cinnamon stick
1 green candle

the ritual

Slice your pumpkin in half. If it's really small, just cut the stem end off as if you were carving a pumpkin. Scoop out all of the flesh and seeds. Rub your pumpkin in your oil. Rub it around the inside and the outside. Focus on abundance and prosperity. Feel the money coming to you. Rub every crevice of the pumpkin, even around the top edge.

Fill the bottom half of your pumpkin with honey. Enchant your herbs one by one. Add the herbs to the honey. Sprinkle in the rice. Lastly, add in a splash of mint water, and a few drops of your Money Flow Citrus Oil. Use your cinnamon stick to stir the mixture together clockwise, always keeping your intention in mind. Leave the cinnamon stick in the pumpkin when everything is combined.

Anoint your candle. Carve money signs or whatever abundance symbolism you like. Place your candle in the center of the honey-herb mixture.

Light your candle and, as it burns, say these words:

Pumpkin, pumpkin
Gourd of abundance
With this spicy cinnamon
And herbs of good fortune
I call prosperity to me
And so mote it be!

Let your candle burn down, and leave your pumpkin for 3 days. On the third day, bury your pumpkin.

HEALING

Day: Thursday
Moon Phase: full moon, waxing moon or waning moon
Colors: light blue and dark blue white

Healing can encompass a variety of areas. Whether you are looking to relieve your anxiety, cut cords with a toxic friendship, let go of negative thought patterns or eliminate negative energy from your aura, this section will help you in any kind of healing you are searching for. Of course using magic is not the only way to heal. It is more of a complementary practice in addition to medical, psychological or spiritual healing. Much like the saying goes, mind over matter, using spells to create healing allows for you to harness your own energy to help you down the right path. This section will cover everything from healing baths to salt soaks, letting go spells and cleansing spells. Energetic cleansing, whether for yourself or your home, is important in having a healthy mind and body.

The properties of herbs are similar in herbalism and in magic, but they do not always have the same meaning. Magical correspondences rely more on energetic, vibrational aspects and less on the actual medicinal benefits. You might use sunflowers for healing depression, pumpkins for abundance or magnolia bark for love. There is so much creativity and personal relationship with the plants that plays a role in how these plants will work for you. If you feel drawn to use a certain plant in a spell, look up the meaning. Perhaps you instinctively knew what you needed to use for a spell. Or perhaps there is no magical correspondence to that plant, but you just felt you needed to use it. That's even better. Start quieting your mind and start listening to your inner knowledge.

This section will cover a wide variety of herbs, as the spells include different healing modalities. Some of the main herbs are lemon balm, chamomile, lavender, peppermint, sunflower and aloe vera.

Lemon Balm is a gentle nervine, and it relaxes both the mind and body. Magically, lemon balm can be used for both physical and mental illness. This is one herb that has similar herbal and magical properties. It is associated with water magic, and it will be used in conjunction with baths and other water-based rituals throughout the chapter. It's also great for anxiety blends and dreamwork.

Chamomile is a gentle, relaxing herb that is so safe and gentle even babies and young children can use it. Chamomile is associated with the element of water which is great for healing. The tender, soothing properties will be used in anxiety-reducing spells in this section.

Lavender is one of the most multipurpose plants in both herbalism and magic. You will be using it in many spells, spanning across all the sections. Lavender is soothing, peaceful and relaxing for your entire being. It can be used for dreamwork, sleep spells, reducing stress, anxiety, depression and overall well-being.

Peppermint is a versatile plant that can be used for healing and health. Peppermint for me is a high vibrational, uplifting energy that also has soothing qualities. Think of peppermint tea for tummy aches. It doesn't cause you to relax like lavender or chamomile, but has a calming effect. This works the same for magical uses. You can use peppermint in healing spells to calm an ailment and quickly resolve the issue.

Sunflower is associated with the sun, solar energy and the first two chakras. These relate to strength, grounding and physical energy. Sunflowers grow tall, and thrive in the energy of the sun. We will be using sunflowers for solar infusions and depression remedies.

Aloe Vera is an extremely healing and soothing plant. When cut open, aloe has a slippery, mucilaginous, thick gel. In herbalism this is used to treat skin conditions and internally for stomach issues. Magically, aloe vera can be used for protection, health and water spells. The gel can be used to soothe illness. This is an example of a plant that is chosen based on intuition. Some plants have certain correspondences that may not align with your personal experience with that plant. For me, this is the case for aloe vera and my dealings with it.

ROSEMARY PAIN-FREE RITUAL

This ritual comes from Colima, Mexico, which is renowned for their brujería. I learned it from a family friend who is well versed in brujería. I love trying these rituals as they come from long lines of practicing witches. They are tried and true spells. This spell was designed to relieve pain in any part of the body. Sometimes when a negative energy or entity has attached to you, you may feel a pressure or pain. Many of us are more susceptible to energies latching on to us. You can feel a heavy sensation on your upper back and neck area. If this is emanating from an energetic malady, use this ritual to rid yourself of the discomfort and cleanse your aura of any attached energies. This spell should be done outside as it requires you to use fire.

ingredients
3 sprigs of fresh rosemary
3 sprigs of fresh basil
3 sprigs of fresh rue
White twine or string
Moon Water Self-Heal Spell (page 126)
Small bowl
Bonfire or cauldron

the ritual

Take your fresh herbs and bundle them together. Wrap the stem ends together with twine or string. You can do this ritual for yourself or another person, or have a partner do this on you.

Pour a small amount of moon water into your bowl. Take the bundle and dip it in moon water. Holy water is traditionally used in brujería; I don't use it, and I substitute moon water. You can also use any other kind of blessed water or even crystal elixirs. Begin to rub the affected area with the bundle dipped in moon water. Don't be afraid to rub vigorously.

Focus on getting rid of the pain. If it is a negative energy that has attached to you, imagine it lifting away as a cloud of smoke and dissipating into the air. Feel lighter, and imagine a weight literally lifting off of you. You feel light as a feather.

Do this for about 3 minutes, then gather any pieces of herb that might have fallen onto the floor. Collect the herb bundle and the pieces and burn them. If you have a firepit or place outdoors to burn them, toss them on the flames. If all you have is a cauldron, toss your herbs in the cauldron and burn them. Any negativity that has attached itself to you is gone. The spell is complete. You will feel relief.

CHAMOMILE
ANXIETY-FREE OIL

Anxiety can be a complicated issue. It is a symptom of a deeper, underlying cause. Many times we are working through issues in therapy, or we might not even be aware of the root cause—but we feel the effects. Anxiety can be truly debilitating. It may be difficult to deal with daily life and you feel overwhelmed. This anxiety oil can be used on a daily basis, to help during a panic attack or after a traumatic event. Make a larger batch and pour some into smaller bottles if you want to keep it with you in your bag, on your desk or by your bed. This oil truly works like magic.

ingredients
Small jar with a lid
3 tbsp (9 g) dried lavender
3 tbsp (6 g) dried lemon balm
3 tbsp (6 g) dried chamomile
3 tbsp (6 g) dried rose petals
1 tbsp (2 g) dried passionflower
1 tbsp (7 g) frankincense
1-inch (2.5-cm) piece of vanilla bean (or vanilla extract/paste)
½ cup (120 ml) sunflower or other plant-based oil
7 drops lavender essential oil
5 drops grapefruit essential oil
Optional: blue lace agate, clear quartz, fluorite or amethyst chips or small tumbled stones
1 white candle
1 light blue candle
1 silver candle

the ritual

Lay out your herbs on your altar or workspace. Have your jar in front of you. Place each herb into the jar one by one. You can crumble and crush the herbs between your fingers as you add them. Focus on feeling calm, relaxed and healthy. You are at peace.

Once all your herbs are in the jar, fill it with the sunflower oil. Add in the essential oils. Make sure the oil goes about an inch (2.5 cm) above the herbs. Add your crystals to the jar (if using) and cover it with a lid. Place the three candles in a pyramid formation around your jar.

Light the candles. Say these words aloud, or if you wish you can just say them in your mind:

Free me of my anxieties
Free me of my fears and worries
May this oil bring me happiness
May it bring me health
Energy and vitality
So mote it be

Let your candles burn down while concentrating on feeling relaxed and at ease. You have nothing to worry about. Once your spell is done, let your oil macerate for a full moon cycle. Once the oil is ready you can dab this on your temples, smell it straight out of the bottle, add it to a bath or even add some into a spray bottle with water.

ROSE SELF-HEALING RITUAL

There are times in life where things might not be manifesting for you the way you want them to. We carry a lot of past unhealed traumas: These can be small traumas or large-scale life-altering events that scar us for life. Sometimes our hearts break in ways that do not allow us to find a healthy relationship with ourselves and with others. We feel stuck and unable to find a way out. You don't need to be fully healed to bring good things to your life, but being on the path to heal yourself—mind, body and soul—requires that you take a step in the right direction. Once you begin the process, you will see all kinds of things in your life unfolding that you never thought possible. Do this spell whenever you feel stuck in an unhealthy cycle. When you see the same toxic behaviors or relationships popping up in your life, look inside to affect change on the physical realm. This gentle, powerful spell will help kick-start that deep healing within.

ingredients
Incense (any kind you prefer)
1 white pillar or taper candle
Lavender Healing Oil (page 134) or a plant-based oil
1 white plate or dish
1 white rose or magnolia flower
5 lavender wands
3 sprigs of fresh sage
3 sprigs of fresh mint
3 sprigs of fresh rosemary
Piece of paper
Pen

the ritual

When I do healing work, I like to use fresh herbs. Herbs in their fresh form have a vigorous, vibrant energy. They are full of life and potency. There is a lot of potential within their cells to bring us healing. But you can also use dried herbs if that's all you have access to. It won't alter your work in any way; it's just a matter of preference.

To begin, light any incense of your choice. Something that makes you feel relaxed and at peace. Try lavender, rose, chamomile or lemon balm.

Anoint your candle with your oil. While you rub the oil across the candle, focus on the healing you want to bring into your life. Think about whatever is holding you back mentally or physically. Begin to imagine a white light entering you and pushing out any dark, negative energy, letting go of any bad memories or negative self-talk.

Place the candle in the center of your dish. Enchant your herbs one by one. Hold them in your hand and speak to them the healing work you want them to do. Scatter each herb around your candle. Once all your herbs are on the dish, write down what you seek healing from on your piece of paper.

I, (your name) am healed
I am healed in my mind, my body, my soul and my heart
May I be healed
To let in love, peace, light and understanding
May I gain a clearer view to
Help guide me along my journey
My physical body is healed
My spirit is healed
My heart is healed
So it is done

Say this intention aloud as you fold the paper three times toward you. Place this paper under your dish. Light your candle. Sit with your candle and imagine what your life will be like now that you are on your path to self-healing. Imagine all the things you can do now that you are no longer held back. The road will begin to open up for you to experience everything you have wanted.

PEPPERMINT HEALING POWDER

Healing is such a broad term but, in magic, healing powders and oils can be used for a variety of purposes and this powder is great to have in your collection. I love having all the oils, powders and herbal blends ready to use whenever I need them. Use this healing powder to rub on your candles, to anoint yourself, to sprinkle over other spell work or to do healing work for other people. Every herb used in this powder is for healing but each one has a specific purpose. Some are for soothing your mind, some for energetic healing and some for physical pain. It can even be mixed with a little oil in a pinch if you run out of other magic oils.

ingredients
Peppermint, lavender, sage or rosemary incense

Mortar and pestle

3 tbsp (6 g) dried sage

3 tbsp (6 g) dried eucalyptus

3 tbsp (9 g) dried lavender

3 tbsp (6 g) dried pink rose petals

3 tbsp (6 g) dried angelica

3 tbsp (10 g) dried rosemary

3 tbsp (6 g) dried peppermint

Small bowl

Small jar with a lid

Optional: 1 fluorite crystal and 1 clear quartz crystal

1 white candle

the ritual

Light your incense. Place each herb in your mortar. Tell the herbs how you want them to work for you. Focus on your intention for this powder. Grind the herbs one by one and add them to your bowl. When all your herbs are powdered, mix them together in the bowl.

To cleanse your jar, pass it through the smoke of your incense. Fill the inside of the jar with smoke and let it flow out naturally. Pour the powder mixture into the jar. Add in your two crystals if you are using them. Cap the jar.

Melt your candle to the lid of your jar. Light the candle and let it burn down. Your powder is now ready to use!

IVY GOOD HEALTH SPELL

Some plants are overlooked for their magical properties because they are so common, or
we just don't understand their more ethereal properties. Ivy is a good example of this. Ivy
is easily found in almost all climates and you can find many varieties in garden centers. Ivy
also has many magical properties. It is often used in health-related spell work because it
represents a long, everlasting life. Ivy grows up walls and trees, giving it tenacity and strong,
vital energy. If you or someone you know is dealing with health issues, you can use the
healing energy of ivy. Always be open to the world of magic. You never know where you
might find healing.

ingredients
1 light blue candle or a blue floating candle
Lavender Healing Oil (page 134) or a plant-based oil
1 tbsp (2 g) dried eucalyptus
1 tbsp (2 g) dried peppermint
Salt
Small cup
Small bowl
Water
8- to 12-inch (20- to 30-cm) piece of ivy

the ritual

To begin, carve on the candle the person's name for which the healing is intended. If it is for yourself, you can carve your name or any healing symbol or words you want to use. Rub a small amount of oil all over the candle. As you rub the oil, imagine yourself healed. As the oil goes over the candle, so the healing will cover your body. Sprinkle the candle with the dried herbs.

Place the salt in the bottom of your small cup. Place your candle in the center of the salt. Make sure the candle can stand on its own. If not, add more salt until it is stable. If you are using a floating candle, sprinkle some of the salt into the water.

Fill your bowl halfway with water and add the small cup with the candle to the center. Place the sprig of ivy around your bowl or in the water, whatever feels right to you.

Light the candle. Focus on the person, or yourself, healed. See the person up and about, walking, laughing and in good health. Say these words aloud over the candle:

Ivy, tenacious and resilient
Bring me (or name of person) healing
Release me from this pain
With these soothing herbs
Good health shall I gain

Continue to focus on healing and charge the candle until it has burned down. The salt will help absorb any illness afflicting the person.

SALT AND SAGE
QUARTZ DETOX

This detox ritual is done in the form of a foot soak. This should be done whenever you feel like a negative entity has attached itself to you. If you feel ill, or depressed out of nowhere, perhaps some kind of spell work has been done to you. You need to detox that toxic energy from your system. Leaving the water in the sun all day infuses the water with the strong, vibrant energy of the sun's rays. Sun water is great to use for depression or low energy.

ingredients
Bucket or small tub

Water

1 cup (292 g) sea salt or Himalayan salt

1 large quartz crystal

Incense (lavender or sage are good here)

3 lavender wands

3 sprigs of fresh sage

the ritual

The morning before you do this ritual, fill your bucket with water. Add your salt and place your quartz in the bucket. Leave the bucket in the sun all day. Once you are ready to do the ritual, bring the bucket indoors or, if possible, do the ritual right outside.

Light your incense. Use a healing herb you like or an incense that is calming and cleansing to you. Add in your lavender wands and sage.

Place your feet in the tub and soak for about 20 minutes. Let go of any thoughts. Meditate if you can, just release all worries. Imagine the water absorbing any negativity, any toxic energy, that has attached itself to you. The infused water pulls the toxins out of your body.

When you are done, take the water outside and throw it into the earth. The earth neutralizes the energy and disperses it. You should feel lighter, clearer and content. You can do this ritual several times, if needed.

MOON WATER
SELF-HEAL SPELL

Moon water is one of my favorite things to make. It is so versatile you can use it for almost anything. If a spell calls for water, you can amp up the energy and use moon water. Add some to your beverage blends, anoint your tools, add it to a bath or cleanse your crystals with it. For this spell, we use moon water for healing, and we want to charge this water with the intention of bringing self-healing. Use water from the most natural source possible: spring water is fantastic. If all you have is bottled water, it's okay. If you don't plan on drinking this, if you use rainwater or melted snow, all the better! This recipe is a basic one, but if you want to add herbs to it, which is my own take on moon water, you can add those as well.

ingredients
Large jar or bowl

Water

Optional: fresh angelica, lemon balm, peppermint or rose petals

Clear quartz crystal

Selenite crystal

Moonstone crystal

Chalice

the ritual

This ritual can be done during any phase of the moon, but I recommend you do this during a full moon. During this time the energy of the moon is at its most potent. You can do this with either a jar or bowl. If you plan on drinking this water, use a jar so nothing falls into it. If you want to use this for other kinds of spell work, just use a bowl.

On the full moon, fill your jar or bowl with water and place it outside. If you want to add some herbs, add those in now. If you are using a jar, cover it with the lid. Place all your crystals around the bowl or on the lid of the jar.

Really focus your energy on healing. If you need physical healing for an illness or relief from emotional issues, state what you want to heal within yourself. Lay your hands over the water and say these words.

I ask you moon
To bless this water
With your divine energies
Give this water the power
To heal and grant me
Good health from
The top of my head to
The toes on my feet

Let the water sit overnight. In the morning, take some of the water and place it in your chalice. Reserve the rest. You will shower yourself with the remaining water. You can do this outdoors or in the privacy of your shower.

When you are ready, hold the bowl over your head and say these words: "Stars above, earth below, heal my _____ (what you need healing for)." Slowly pour the moon water over you. Repeat this phrase until you run out of moon water. Once you have dried off, drink the chalice of moon water.

SUNFLOWER DEPRESSION POTION

Sun water is something I like to drink when I feel melancholy or depressed. Many times we can have hormonal imbalances or situational sadness that causes us to feel blue for no reason, so it seems. Clinical depression is one of the most difficult things to deal with. If you have it or have been through it, you will know the depths of despair that you fall into. Magic is not a cure for depression. But it is a tool you can use to help alleviate some of the symptoms or, even better, help you on the road out of those depths. When I was really struggling in my early twenties, on days where it was difficult to just leave my room, the sun is what really helped save me. I know that is not all it takes—but sitting outside for ten minutes in the sun can shift something. Infusing the energy of the sun into your water warms your soul. It brings the energy of strength, vitality and vigor, the very life force that keeps us all alive. Use this potion when you feel like you are slipping down into that dark hole. If you are in the throes of depression, you can drink this daily to help get you to a place where you can begin to heal.

ingredients
Large glass jar

2–3 sprigs of fresh lemon balm

2–3 sprigs of fresh peppermint

3–5 lavender stems

Handful of fresh rose petals

Handful of fresh sunflower petals or calendula

Water

Tray or large plate

Carnelian crystal

Citrine crystal

Tiger's eye crystal

the ritual

Place your jar on your workspace. Enchant each herb one by one. Say these words out loud to each plant: "Heal me, bring me happiness, bring me joy, alleviate my spirit." Use whatever words represent healing depression to you. Close your eyes and focus on feeling happy. If you can't imagine that, just imagine as close to it as you can. Imagine a happy memory or something that makes you laugh. Smile. Place the herbs into the jar like this one by one.

Fill the jar with water. You will drink this so make sure to use the most natural water possible, but bottled or filtered is fine. This is kind of like making sun tea and a flower essence in one.

Place the jar on a tray, and place the crystals around the jar. You can leave this in a sunny window or, even better, outside. Leave the jar open to the sun. Leave it outside for about 10 minutes. You don't want to heat the water, just infuse it with the energy of the sun's rays.

After 10 minutes, sit outside with the jar. Place your hands over the jar and again focus on that feeling of joy. Slowly sip the water as you bask in the sun.

Make this part of your everyday routine. Making this a special time during your day to break that negative energy and do something different helps your mood.

LEMON BALM
HEALING BATH

All baths are healing. Water is a powerful source of life and full of healing energy: Taking a dip in the ocean, a river or a swimming hole can completely revitalize you. Many indigenous and religious practices involve saying a prayer over water to imbue it with the intention to provide healing. There is a long history of the curative power of water. The different baths in this book have specific ingredients to bring different forms of healing, but it's all about the intention and the tools you use for each bath. The words you speak into the water become your intentions and thus the beneficial healing energy.

ingredients
Handful of fresh lemon balm
Handful of fresh peppermint
10–12 sprigs of fresh rosemary
8–10 fresh elderflower heads
3–5 lemons, sliced
3–5 oranges, sliced
Clear quartz crystal
Fluorite crystal
1 cup (292 g) sea salt
Light blue and white candles

the ritual

This bath can be made with either fresh or dried herbs. Elderflowers are only available in the spring, while the other ingredients can be grown or purchased year round—so it's up to you. You can also use all fresh herbs and substitute dried elderflowers if you are doing this ritual during other seasons.

To begin, clean your bathroom where you will be soaking. Make sure it is free of clutter and debris. Set the mood for your ritual bath. Fill your tub with water. Place each herb one by one into your tub.

As you place each herb into the water say: "I ask you (name of herb) to grant me your healing powers."

Close your eyes and focus on feeling better. Whatever it is you desire healing from, whether physical or mental, focus on the feeling of health and well-being.

Next, add the fruit and your crystals into the water along with the salt. Light your candles and get in. Soak for about 20 minutes. Try to let go of any thoughts and worries. You should also dip your head in. Cover your entire body with the water. Feel relieved knowing that healing is on its way.

BIRCH TREE
LETTING GO SPELL

Learning to let go can be difficult. Many times you hold on to something, whether that's a toxic relationship, old patterns, negative self-talk or bad habits—and you get stuck. You are not changing and evolving to be the best you possible. This can cause anxiety, stress and tension in the body that seems to come out of nowhere. I love doing these spells when I want to let go of something that is no longer serving me. Letting go can sound drastic, but like the old saying goes you need to let go if something is truly meant for you. To create change and shake up your energy, you need to let go of what is not creating happiness and growth in your life. This spell can be done in two different ways. Choose the one that appeals to you the most.

ingredients
Version 1
7 pieces of dried birch bark
1 white tealight candle
Marker
Cauldron

Version 2
7 small birch twigs
1 white tealight candle

the ritual

This first version is a more traditional letting go spell that involves you writing down specific things you want to let go of and burning them. Instead of using paper, you will be using birch bark. Birch bark is often used to write down wishes to have them come true. So, while you are letting go of something, it is a positive representation of new beginnings and better things to come.

Make sure you are using bark from a fallen branch. You don't want to damage the tree. Let the bark dry for about a week before using it. If you can't find birch bark, you can do this with a bay leaf or a leaf from the same tree.

Light your candle. Write what you want to let go of on the bark. You can write down seven different aspects of the specific issue you are focusing on, or seven different things you are trying to let go of. Focus intently on what is no longer serving you. Take each piece of bark in your hands and focus on this. Take each piece one by one and light the edge with the candle. Drop it into your cauldron and let it burn. When you are done, you can throw the ashes into the earth.

The second version was inspired by a ritual I did with my best friend near a river. It worked very well. You can do this by a river, stream or the ocean. You need a source of running water. Collect your twigs. They should preferably be birch, but you can use oak, maple or ash—whatever trees grow in your area.

To begin, light your candle and set your intentions. What are you looking to let go of? What negative feelings or emotions are you letting go of with that event, person or pattern?

Take each twig and imagine the thing you want out of your life. Close your eyes and hold the twig between your hands. Focus your energy into that twig. When you are ready, take the twig and hold it over the candle until it breaks in half. Do this with all seven twigs. Take each broken piece of twig and throw it into the water. As the twigs float away from you, so does all the negative energy. It is done, you are free.

LAVENDER HEALING OIL

Healing is not always for a physical malady. Often we seek healing from a broken relationship, a loss, depression or the physical manifestations of illness. All systems of our body, including the spiritual and physical, are working together in unison. What goes on in the mind manifests in the physical realm. This is why many times when you are depressed you might experience back pain or headaches. Anxiety can cause heart palpitations or upset stomachs. When you need true healing, magic oils hold a high vibration to help heal you. Use this to anoint yourself, your candles and your tools; or use it as part of other ritual work.

ingredients
Purifying incense
Small jar with a lid
Mortar and pestle
3 tbsp (9 g) dried lavender or 3 lavender wands
3 tbsp (6 g) dried lemon balm
3 tbsp (10 g) dried rosemary
3 tbsp (6 g) dried eucalyptus
3 tbsp (6 g) dried peppermint
7 cloves
7 juniper berries
Pinch of sea salt
Sunflower or other plant-based oil
1 small white candle

the ritual

Light your incense. Begin by cleansing your bottle or jar that you will be placing your oil into. You can use any purifying incense or herb. If you like you can also use a lavender wand if you are using whole lavender for this oil. Make sure you get inside as well as outside the bottle. Blow a little of your breath into the bottle.

In your mortar, you will grind each herb. You don't need them to be a powder; you are going to release all the beautiful essential oils, so that they can infuse into the carrier oil.

State your intention for this oil. You will enchant each herb as you place it into the mortar. You can whisper words such as "healing," "heal me," "grant me health" or "good health" across the herbs as you hold them in your hands.

Repeat these words as you move your pestle clockwise. It is important to do this for each herb, not just to toss everything in at once and get it over with. This is part of the magical process. Time should be taken on each herb to properly enchant it. After you process each herb, place it in your jar. Add in your pinch of sea salt.

Once your jar is full of your herbs, top it off with your oil and cover it with a lid.

Inscribe your candle with similar words you used for enchanting your herbs. You can write health, or use symbols that represent healing to you. Melt the bottom of the candle and place it on top of the jar. Let the candle melt down. Let your oil infuse for one full moon cycle before using it.

SAGE GROUNDING RITUAL

Have you ever felt foggy with sensations of being out of reality? Whether it's brought on by stress or a more severe reason, such as anxiety, panic or PTSD, we often lack clarity. Some people also need a lot of grounding—those who are highly sensitive or creative, or even air signs who often have their heads in the clouds. If you have experienced these sensations before or feel this way all the time, you know exactly what I am referring to. It might take a while to fully heal from these conditions, through therapy and a lot of work. But if you want to feel a little more tethered to this reality, then this spell is for you. It can also be done if you are in a high-stress situation and simply want to get a handle on it with a clear head. Feel free to substitute herbs that you find grounding. Using roots and tree medicine—leaves, bark, fruit—is extremely grounding!

ingredients
Metal, wood or ceramic tray or plate

1 brown candle

Boline or knife

Handful of dirt

¼ cup (8 g) dried eucalyptus

¼ cup (13 g) dried rosemary

¼ cup (6 g) dried peppermint

¼ cup (12 g) dried lavender

¼ cup (6 g) dried sage

¼ cup (32 g) dried birch bark

Hematite crystal

Smoky quartz crystal

Obsidian crystal

the ritual

To perform this ritual, it is absolutely necessary to do this outdoors. You need to do this in a place where you can be barefoot in the dirt. Our connection to mother earth fades when we protect our feet with socks and shoes. Our ancestors spent the majority of their time outdoors, feeling that connection all the time. The more time we spend indoors with electronic devices the more we begin to lose that precious connection. As a modern society we experience anxiety in such astounding numbers because of our lifestyle.

So to begin, go to a place where you feel comfortable and safe, where no one will intrude on your ritual. If I could only tell you the story of the time a friend and I were "caught" by some park rangers doing a spell . . . and the explanations we had to give to not look like total weirdos. . . . You want to feel safe and have privacy to do this. If the only access you have to nature is your own yard or a local park, this is fine too.

Once you find your special place outside, remove your shoes. Stand for 5 minutes just feeling the grass or dirt between your toes. How does this feel? Close your eyes and stand up straight. Feel the connection between you and the earth. Imagine your feet growing roots. Picture those roots growing farther and farther down into the earth. Feel that connection. Once you feel securely rooted, sit down.

Set your tray or plate on the ground. Take your candle and carve these words into it: "I am grounded. I am rooted. I am safe and secure." Set the candle in the center of your tray. Sprinkle the dirt around your candle. If there is moss, fallen leaves or twigs around you, feel free to add anything you like to the dirt.

Take each herb and hold it between your hands. Keep repeating the words you carved on your candle: "I am grounded. I am rooted. I am safe and secure."

Do this with each herb and add it around your candle. Add your crystals. Crystals come from the earth and are highly grounding, so if you have more than one, add as many as you can.

Sit with the candle until it burns down. Feel the connection to the earth. After this ritual, make sure you take the time to practice grounding every day. Go outside for 5 to 10 minutes each day to stand in the earth and rooting. Slowly the fog will begin to lift, and you will feel more anchored.

ALOE VERA HEALING SPELL

This spell can be used on yourself or done for someone else. Aloe vera is used in herbalism and in magic for its healing properties. It is commonly used for skin issues, but can also be consumed internally as a juice. It works on so many levels that it is one of the best plants to use for healing. It can be found pretty easily in many ethnic grocery stores. If you don't already have some growing in your magic garden, it is so easy to grow. It also constantly makes new babies; you'll soon have enough plants to share.

ingredients
Scrap of brown paper
Pen
1 aloe vera leaf
Boline or small knife
3-foot (91-cm)-long piece of white string
Small bowl
Water
1 tbsp (2 g) dried calendula
1 tbsp (3 g) dried rosemary
1 tbsp (2 g) dried peppermint
3 light blue candles

the ritual

Get a scrap of brown paper. Tear the paper into a small square, big enough to write a few sentences. Focus on what you intend to heal. This should be something more physical than mental.

On one side of the paper write these words:

Soothing aloe vera
Bring my body healing
Renew me, restore me
Back to perfect health
I feel strong, I feel energy
I feel completely healed

On the reverse side, write your name three times. If you are doing this for someone else, write their name. Turn the paper to the right, and over your name write "I am healed" three times. Turn the paper once more clockwise and sign your name three times. Fold the paper toward you, turn it clockwise, fold it toward you and once more. Once you have the paper folded into a small square, set it aside.

Take the aloe vera leaf in your hand and repeat the chant above three times. Focus on feeling healed. Take your knife and carefully slice the aloe in half lengthwise. Place your paper square between the two slices.

Take a length of your white string about 3 feet (91 cm) long. Begin winding the string around the aloe, binding the two halves together. Make sure you are pulling it toward you. You want to usher in good health.

Close your eyes and really feel the energy. You can repeat these words over and over: I am healed. Once the aloe is bound, tie it off. Place the aloe in your small bowl. Slowly pour the water over it, imagining a healing white light. Sprinkle the other herbs into the water while repeating "I am healed, I am healed. . . ."

Surround your bowl with the three candles. Carve your name or the person's name into them. Light the candles, while focusing on feeling restored and a feeling of well-being. Let the candles burn down.

CHAMOMILE FRIENDSHIP MEND SPELL

I've placed this spell in the health section because, let's face it, issues in relationships can cause anxiety and stress. When you and a friend just don't see eye to eye, the miscommunication can cause a rift. Maybe they are still in your life, or you have stopped talking and you want to draw them back and heal the relationship. Or your friend may have hurt your feelings, and you want to convey how you feel without starting an argument. You want to open the channel for clear communication—have the other person really see your side and understand you. This spell helps you mend your friendship so you can truly be open with the other person and move forward in peace.

ingredients
3 tbsp (6 g) dried passionflower
3 tbsp (9 g) dried lavender
3 tbsp (18 g) dried lemon peel
3 tbsp (6 g) dried chamomile
3 tbsp (6 g) dried calendula
Mortar and pestle
Small bowl
3 tbsp (45 g) granulated sugar
1 pink or orange candle
Lavender Healing Oil (page 134) or a plant-based oil
Tray or plate
Lapis lazuli
Oven-dry clay (pink, orange or transparent)

the ritual

For this spell, you will be making a friendship charm. It can be made into a necklace or kept on your person. If this is a friendship that is still intact, you can give one half to your friend. If you are trying to draw back an ex-friend, then you can make the charm and keep it for yourself.

Place each herb between your hands as you enchant them for friendship. Imagine a healing between you two. There is no more arguing or resentment. You have opened up a path of clear communication where there are no misunderstandings. Lightly crush each of the herbs in your mortar, and place them in your bowl.

Take a pinch of the herb mixture, and mix it with the sugar. Anoint your candle with oil. Roll the candle in the sugar-herb mixture over your tray. Place your candle in the center of your plate or tray. Sprinkle the remaining herbs around the candle. Place the lapis lazuli stone next to the candle.

Take a small pinch of the remaining herb and mix it into your clay. You need a small amount of clay, enough to form a small heart. Mix the herbs and clay together. Flatten your clay between your fingers, forming a heart shape. If you will be giving your friend half, cut the heart in half. If you will be keeping it, leave it intact. Bake the charm according to your directions on your clay.

Place your charm next to your candle. Light the candle and let it burn. As it burns, imagine you and your friend reuniting, smiling and happy. Infuse this energy into the charm. As the candle burns, your charm is charging with the intent for reconciliation.

Keep the charm and the crystal together until your friend returns. If you want to give your friend half, do so. No need to let them know of the magical intentions behind it. Whether they wear it or keep it in their house, it will still work.

PERSONAL POWER

Days: Tuesday and Wednesday
Moon Phase: full moon, new moon or waxing moon
Colors: orange, red and yellow

While most spells tend to focus on attracting or banishing, few focus on your own personal power. Often, we lack confidence to believe in our spell work, or we need to unleash our intuition or magical abilities. This section concentrates on the different ways you can direct your own power and strength. Have you ever done a spell and as time passes you begin to lose confidence that it will work? Do you want to know how to add fire and speed up spells? Want to open your third eye and get in touch with your intuition? This chapter will help you become the most self-confident, powerful witch that can manifest anything you set your mind to!

The herbs that you will focus on in this section are frankincense, dragon's blood, lemon peel, star anise and sandalwood.

Frankincense is the ultimate magical ingredient. It adds that extra boost in any spell you do. It is a resin that comes from the *Boswellia* genus of tree. It has been used since ancient times as an incense and herbal medicine. It is extremely powerful. It is ruled by the element of the sun and can be used as an offering for any gods. It is used to raise the energy in preparation for or during spell work. You can use frankincense in all kinds of magic; it is a powerful cleanser, brings good fortune and can be added in any type of ritual where you want that extra element of power.

Dragon's Blood is another kind of resin that has a deep red hue. It has been used throughout history as a dye, medicine and incense. It comes in large chunks that you can powder in your mortar. It will turn any oil a beautiful red color. Dragon's blood is similar to frankincense in that it will add an element of power. You can use the powder to create ink to write spells, enhance any oil or powder, and even bring back a lost love. It can be used for protection, energizing, love, increasing potency and, of course, enhancing your personal power.

Lemon Peel gives off a bright, energetic and cleansing energy. While lemon is most commonly thought of for cleansing and purifying, it is also excellent for spiritual matters. Lemon is great for spiritual awakening. It opens your intuition and cleanses your aura. Lemon, along with all other citrus fruits, is a highly energizing, uplifting energy. This makes it perfect for a ritual bath before any of these personal power spells.

Star Anise also assists in enhancing the power in your spells. It can be used for any kind of divination work and helps open your psychic ability. This is a great herb to add to any spells where you will be doing dreamwork or divination and want to protect yourself.

Sandalwood is another ancient wood that has long been used in incense and perfume blends. It is a divine herb used to create peace and a meditative state. It opens your intuition and psychic powers. It is a spiritual incense that can be used to call upon deities in your workings or to use as an offering. It is important to note that sandalwood should be used sparingly. It is now endangered, and the only current sustainable option comes from Australia (*Santalum spicatum*). Do not buy from Indian sandalwood trees as those species are endangered.

FRANKINCENSE POWER
ENHANCEMENT OIL

This ceremonial oil is designed for you to intensify the intent behind your spells. It contains herbs that empower you, give you courage, enhance your intuition, improve your focus and give you strength. There are days when you don't feel your best and need a little help. Or perhaps you want to add an extra boost of energy to your spells. This oil is sort of a fragrance you can dab on yourself before you do any spell work. You can feel this oil as soon as you rub it on your hands. It is almost electric, vibrating with such a high energy. This recipe calls for sunflower oil which has strengthening properties, but you can substitute any oil you have on hand.

ingredients

Sandalwood incense
Small jar with a lid
Small bowl
. 1 tbsp (7 g) frankincense
1 tbsp (2 g) sunflower petals
1 tbsp (6 g) dried orange peel
1 tbsp (6 g) dried lemon peel
1 tbsp (2 g) dried lemon verbena
1 tbsp (5 g) dried lemongrass
1 tbsp (4 g) juniper berries
1 tbsp (4 g) whole cloves

1 cinnamon stick or 1 tbsp (8 g)
cinnamon chips
3 star anise
Optional: citrine, sunstone,
carnelian or tiger's eye crystals
½ cup (120 ml) sunflower or other
plant-based oil
1 orange candle
1 yellow candle
1 red candle

the ritual

Light your incense and cleanse your jar in the smoke. Fill the inside with smoke, then hold it above the incense and let it envelop the jar. Set the jar aside and let it air out.

One by one, place your herbs into your bowl. Lay your hands over the bowl and enchant the herbs one at a time. Ask them to grant you power and strength.

Once all the herbs are in the bowl, you can also let the smoke cleanse the herbs. Mix them well with your hands, all the while focusing on your intention for this oil to bring you more personal power and mental agility.

Pour the herbs into the jar. If you are using any crystals, add them in. Top the jar with sunflower oil and cover it with a lid.

On your altar or workspace, place the three candles around the jar. Light the candles and let them burn down. Leave this oil to sit for a full moon cycle before using it.

CITRUS ENERGIZING BATH

This bath uses storm water—rainwater collected during a storm. It has the ability to clear blockages, give you strength and energize you. You can use this before any ritual work to make sure you feel strong and able to do the work, or use it on any day when you need to feel that extra boost. I like to use fresh herbs whenever I do health spells or anything for empowerment. They have that vital life force, and it feels natural to use them in their fresh form. If you use dried, it won't make this ritual any less effective.

ingredients
Large stockpot
7 sprigs of fresh peppermint
7 sprigs of fresh rosemary
7 sprigs of fresh sage
3 cups (720 ml) storm water
3 oranges
3 lemons
3 limes
Citrine, carnelian, tiger's eye, sunstone or any orange or yellow crystals
Yellow or orange candles

the ritual

Begin by making your bath area nice and tidy. Clear any mess, and make sure your tub and space are clean. Clean the area energetically by using a cleansing herb such as sage or lavender as incense.

While your tub is filling, in a stockpot add your peppermint, rosemary and sage; enchant each herb before you add it. Fill the pot with storm water. Let the herbs steep in the pot, stirring it occasionally. Let the herbs infuse for about 10 minutes. You can strain the herbs out at this point and leave them in your garden for compost.

Slice your oranges, lemons and limes. We will be adding this into your bath.

Once your bath is ready, add your herb water to the bath. Place each citrus fruit one by one into the bath, remembering your intention of personal power. You can add your crystals into the bath water or around the edge of the tub. Light your candles.

Submerge into the water for 20 to 30 minutes. Feel the water physically energizing you. Imagine yourself surrounded by a bright white pulsating light. You are alive and vibrant with energy. You are now ready to handle whatever comes your way today or ready to do your spell work.

QUICK BOOST COFFEE POWDER

Have you ever wondered if you can speed up or enhance a spell? Perhaps you have a bill due or need a response by a certain date, or you want to add some power to a love spell. If you have a deadline or are under any kind of time constraint, you add this powder to a spell. Use this to anoint candles or to pour over a spell, or you can even add a little oil and rub it on yourself before a ritual. Coffee is used across different folk magic traditions to speed up or add energy to a spell. If you want something to move faster, have this powder on hand.

ingredients
Mortar and pestle
1 tbsp (7 g) dragon's blood
1 tbsp (7 g) frankincense
3 tbsp (23 g) ground cinnamon
1 tsp chili powder
¼ cup (12 g) ground coffee
Small bowl
Small jar with a lid
1 gold candle

the ritual

For this recipe, you can grind the spices yourself or use them already ground. If you buy your coffee already ground that will work, but I have used my mortar to crush coffee when that's all I had. It's up to you. If you are grinding them yourself, enchant each spice as you work the pestle in a clockwise motion. Empower these spices to hasten your workings.

Place the ground spices in a bowl. Mix them until they're fully combined. Place the powder into your jar.

To energize this powder, I like to use a gold candle. If you feel called to use red or yellow you can do that as well, but gold has a special feel to it. Light your gold candle on top of your jar. Let it burn as you focus on speed and knowing that your spells will work quickly. No matter the deadline, you will get it done!

LEMON BALM CLARITY SPELL

Use this spell when you are seeking clarity. Even if you feel your intuition is strong, there are times where you feel lost and confused. Maybe you are unsure of which direction to go in. Maybe you let the opinions of friends and family fog your own vision. It can be difficult to always be clearheaded and know what to do in any given situation. If you have anxiety, this ritual will help you focus your mind, clear out the external voices and come to a decision.

ingredients
Water

1 large bowl

Cinnamon incense

1 yellow candle

1 tbsp (6 g) fresh lemongrass

1 tbsp (6 g) fresh peppermint

1 tbsp (6 g) fresh lemon balm

Teacup

the ritual

Gather your herbs. Try and use fresh if you can find them. Pour the water into your bowl. Light your cinnamon incense. Light your yellow candle.

If you are using fresh herbs, hold them together in a bundle and run them over your bowl of water. Let the tips of the herbs skim over the top of the water, moving in a clockwise motion. Do this three times.

Make a tea using the herbs. Gaze into the bowl of water as you say these words:

> *As this water is crystal clear*
> *Let my mind be free of clutter*
> *Grant me insight*
> *And clarity*

Stare into the bowl of water for 10 to 15 minutes. As any thoughts of doubt or confusion come up, acknowledge them and let them flow into the bowl. Focus on how clear and pure the water is and how soon your mind will be clear and pure.

Once your tea is cool enough to drink, sip it, knowing you will soon come to a decision.

MULLEIN DIVINATION WASH

Most, if not all, witches have done some form of divination in their practice. This can be tarot card readings, tea leaf readings, runes, scrying, working with pendulums and palmistry. There are so many types of divination you can try. Different magical practices use shells, bones, egg yolks, apple seeds and corn among other things to predict the future. While we can cleanse our tools with smoke or bury them in salt, this herbal wash is perfect for cleansing both your tools and your hands before you begin. If you do readings for other people, this is a good ritual you can do before beginning your work. You can also use this blend of herbs to make a divination oil, incense or powder. It is versatile and can be used as the base for many different magical preparations.

ingredients
Large bowl
1 tbsp (2 g) dried mugwort
1 tbsp (2 g) dried sage
1 tbsp (2 g) dried mullein
1 tbsp (3 g) dried rosemary
1 tbsp (5 g) dried lemongrass
1 tbsp (3 g) dried lavender
1 tbsp (6 g) dried orange peel
¼ cup (73 g) sea salt
Splash of mint water
Lukewarm water
Optional: alcohol (vodka or rubbing alcohol)

the ritual

This divination wash is meant to be used right away. You can make this earlier in the day or overnight, but it will not keep. If you want to bottle this and use it as a spray, you can substitute alcohol for the water. Or if you have essential oils, you can swap out the dried herbs for essential oils and add them to the water.

In your large bowl, add each herb in one by one. These are herbs for divination, protection and opening your psychic senses. When you are doing any kind of magical workings you want to be open to possibilities, but always protect yourself. Focus on your intentions and let yourself be open and protected while doing it. Focus on getting the answers you need or want to get, whether it's for you or for clients. This wash is great for people who do tarot or other kinds of divination work for others.

Mix all the herbs together with the salt. Let them run through your fingers as you blend them together. Add in your mint water, and pour the lukewarm water over the herbs. Squeeze the herbs into the water. Do this for about 5 minutes. You can spray this water where you do your divination work, wash your hands with it, sprinkle it on your body and cleanse all your tools with it. Physically wash your tools or sprinkle some on—whatever feels instinctively good to you. If you decided to make this with alcohol or essential oils, you can bottle this up and keep it for later! Happy divining.

RED CLOVER CONFIDENCE GLAMOUR

The purpose of glamour spells or confidence spells is to be—and feel—as comfortable as possible being your authentic self. Confidence is important for everyone and it matters when it comes to magic because you want to be confident when doing your workings. Unfortunately, confidence is often confused with arrogance. You don't have to be conceited to be confident. You don't have to look a certain way or act a certain way to be confident in yourself. But if you don't think highly of yourself how do you expect others to? This spell can be made into an oil, perfume or any other beauty product you can think of.

ingredients

Medium stockpot

¼ cup (60 ml) melted coconut or almond oil

Glass measuring cup

1 tsp dried lemon balm

1 tsp dried rose petals

1 tsp dried red clover

1 tsp dried peppermint

2 tsp (6 g) alkanet root or a piece of your favorite lipstick

1 tbsp (17 g) beeswax

Small glass jar or an empty cosmetics container

Small bowl

Handful of Himalayan salt

Tiger's eye crystal

Carnelian crystal

Rose quartz crystal

1 small orange candle

Frankincense Power Enhancement Oil (page 146) or a plant-based oil

the ritual

For this spell you will be making your own lip balm. It is infused with herbs for confidence. You can infuse the oil ahead of time by putting all the herbs and oil in a jar and letting them sit for a few weeks. You can also achieve this more quickly by heating them over the stove. Fill your pot with a few inches of water and place it over medium heat. Place your coconut oil in your measuring cup. Charge each of your herbs. Stand tall, with shoulders back, and feel strong and confident as you charge each of the herbs. Place all the herbs into the oil. Put your measuring cup into the pot of hot water. Turn it down to low and let this simmer for about 30 minutes. The alkanet root is what gives it color, but if you don't have any, you can also add in a small piece of your favorite lipstick for color. After 30 minutes, strain all the herbs out of the oil. Return the strained oil into the measuring cup and place it in the pot once again.

Add in the beeswax and let it melt. Stir the mixture, enchanting it and energizing it. Once everything has melted, pour it into your container of choice. Let it set up a little bit until the liquid has become opaque.

Add the salt into your small bowl. Place your balm in the center of your bowl of salt. You can add some of the dried herbs into your salt if you wish. Place the crystals around the balm in a pyramid formation.

Engrave the candle with symbols or words that exude confidence to you. Anoint it with oil. Light the candle. As it burns, focus on your energy growing stronger and more confident. Once the candle burns down, your balm is ready to use. Every time you wear this feel that inner confidence shine through. This is also wonderful to use during ritual work or when you need a lot of inner strength.

SANDALWOOD SPELL SUCCESS INCENSE

This incense is designed to be used during any spell work to increase your personal power and success. Feel confident knowing that you possess a great deal of strength and power within you to carry your spells through. Whether you use deities or ancestors in your spells, know that you, too, have influence on these rituals. You can burn this anytime before the ritual to empower you and to instill extra confidence to prepare you for spell work. You can also use this anytime you want an energy boost before going out, meeting with people or any important life events.

ingredients
3 cinnamon sticks
1 tbsp (7 g) dragon's blood
1 tbsp (7 g) frankincense
3 tbsp (14 g) dried basil
3 tbsp (6 g) dried mugwort
3 tbsp (6 g) dried rose petals
1 tbsp (7 g) sandalwood powder
Mortar and pestle
Bowl
Small jar with a lid
1 small orange candle
Frankincense Power Enhancement Oil (page 146) or a plant-based oil

the ritual

Make this incense on a day where you are feeling great. You want to feel confident and powerful. Don't do this when you are feeling sick or with low energy. You will want to put a lot of energy into this one, since you will be using it for success.

Enchant each herb with your intentions: Take each herb in your hands and imagine a bright orange light surrounding it. Feel the energy radiating from your hands. Feel how much energy you will have when burning this incense. Once the herb is ready, place it in your mortar and crush it into smaller pieces. No need to powder this. It just needs to be small enough to evenly burn on a charcoal disc.

Place all your crushed herbs into a bowl and mix them. Always stir them in a clockwise direction. Place the herbs into your jar, and cover it with a lid.

Anoint your candle with Frankincense Power Enhancement Oil or any plant-based oil you like. Place it on the lid of your jar and light it. Let it burn down. Your incense is now ready to use.

ANISE MAGICAL ABILITY AMULET

This amulet takes herbs that enhance your magical abilities and combines them with your own personal power sigil. Making sigils is one of the cornerstones of magic, and creating your own magical symbol is extremely personal. In this case you will be creating a sigil that represents your personal power to carry with you. You can also use this same sigil to engrave into candles or even as a symbol on your altar. It is important that you go into spell work with confidence, and carrying this amulet will ensure that you feel powerful and that your spells will indeed manifest.

ingredients
2 pieces of paper

Red pen or Magical Love Ink (page 78)

Small vial

Personal power incense

1 tsp frankincense

1 tsp sandalwood powder

1 tsp dragon's blood

1 tsp ground cinnamon

1 tsp dried ginger

1 star anise

Mortar and pestle

1 (16-inch [41-cm]) piece of cord or jewelry chain

1 lobster claw clasp (optional)

Pliers (optional)

2 jump rings (optional)

3 purple candles

Frankincense Power Enhancement Oil (page 146) or a plant-based oil

the ritual

The first part of this magical working involves creating your own personal power sigil. To make a sigil, write out a phrase or intention that you want to make into a symbol. For this amulet, you might use one of these phrases: I am a powerful witch or All my spells manifest. Anything that indicates that you have the ability to carry your spells through. Something that inspires you and gives you confidence.

For this example, write "I am a powerful witch" on the first sheet of paper. Go through and cross out any vowels. You will be left with: M P W R F L W T C H.

Go back through and cross out any doubles. In this example there is only one double, which is W. Now you are left with M P W R F L T C H.

You will be transforming these letters into a symbol. Play around with the letters. Draw them as stylized as you like. Keep drawing new versions until you simplify it down into the final form. Draw a circle around this sigil. This is your power symbol.

You can activate this in the same way you visualize your intentions in all other spell work. You can sit with this paper and meditate. You can burn it, leave it under the moon, place a crystal on top or let it dissolve in a glass of water. Once it is activated you can write it anywhere and the power is already held within the symbol.

For the amulet, write your sigil in dragon's blood ink or regular pen ink on a small scrap of the second piece of paper small enough to fit into your vial. Set this aside. Take your vial and cleanse it in the smoke of your incense. Enchant your herbs one by one, focusing on your own inner strength and ability to create magic. Feel the intensity of your own being. Place the herbs one by one into your vial. Use your mortar and pestle to gently crush any herbs that are too big to fit through the vial opening. Lastly add in your sigil. Cap the vial. String the vial onto your cord or chain. If you are using a cord, simply tie the ends into a knot. For the chain, use pliers to attach a lobster claw clasp and a jump ring to one end. Attach a jump ring to the other end.

Carve your sigil into each of the three purple candles. Anoint it with your oil. Arrange your candles in a pyramid shape around your amulet. Light your candles and let them burn down.

Your amulet is now activated and ready to use. Wear this amulet before spell work, or wear it daily if you like. Know your inner strength and power.

HEATHER GOOD LUCK PERFUME

Plant devas, fairies, elementals or nature spirits have a deep history around the world. They open us up to the realm of the unknown and the unseen. Are they real or are they merely ancient ways of making sense of the unfamiliar? Whether you believe in them or not, nature spirits make up the very essence of plants. For this perfume, I have chosen flowers associated with fairies such as heather and lavender.

Heather is a beautiful plant. When you buy it in its dried form it looks like fairy dust: tiny lilac-colored blossoms. Heather is known to bring good luck and confidence, among other properties. The other flowers also help open you up to the physical manifestation of fairies and to all kinds of magic. Wear this perfume when you feel like you need a dose of good luck or want to open yourself to the magic around you.

ingredients
Few drops of morning dew
Large vial or small jar with a lid
3 tbsp (9 g) dried heather flowers
3 tbsp (9 g) dried lavender
3 tbsp (9 g) dried pink roses
1 tbsp (2 g) dried fern
1 tbsp (6 g) dried orange peel
1 small piece of vanilla bean
Splash of orange blossom water or rosewater
½ cup (120 ml) vodka
1 silver candle
Atomizer or perfume bottle

the ritual

This is best done in the early morning or at dusk. It is also great if you can do it outdoors somewhere near flowers or ferns—where the fairies tend to hide.

If you are doing it in the morning, collect your morning dew, giving thanks to the plant spirits for bringing you good luck and blessings. You can put the dew directly into your jar. Place your herbs in one by one, setting your intentions of good luck. You can also ask the fairies to bless your herbs and thank them for their work.

Add your orange blossom water or rosewater, then top off the rest of the jar with vodka. Close your jar and melt your silver candle over top or next to your jar. Light the candle and let it burn all the way down. Make sure to show gratitude for the plants and plant spirits that make nature possible.

Let your perfume sit for a full moon cycle before using it. Transfer your perfume to a spray bottle. Spray this on before you start your day to experience lots of luck, blessings and magic and to open yourself up to the unlimited possibilities!

MUGWORT INTUITION DEVELOPMENT OIL

We all have a sense of intuition. Some of us who are more sensitive or open tend to be more in tune with our own intuition. This oil is designed to be used before doing ritual work, for divination, when reading tarot cards or when you feel like you are out of touch with your inner voice. Some days our intuition can be very strong. Other days we can confuse ourselves, not letting our inner guide show us the way. Oftentimes I confuse my sense of intuition with doubt or I let past negative experiences blur my truth. The secret ingredient in this oil, saffron, has been known to enhance your psychic vision. This oil can be applied to your third eye or anywhere on your body in order to enhance your own intuitive and psychic abilities.

ingredients

Mortar and pestle
1 tbsp (3 g) dried rosemary
1 tbsp (2 g) dried tulsi (holy basil)
1 tbsp (2 g) dried rose petals
1 tbsp (2 g) dried mugwort
1 tbsp (2 g) dried peppermint
1 tbsp (7 g) frankincense
1 tbsp (7 g) dragon's blood
Pinch of saffron

Small jar or bottle with a lid
Amethyst crystal
Labradorite crystal
Clear quartz crystal
1 cup (240 ml) olive or other
plant-based oil
1 purple candle
Optional: Frankincense Power
Enhancement Oil (page 146)

the ritual

Begin by breaking down your herbs. Using your mortar and pestle, crush the herbs until they are finely ground. You don't want these to be powdered, just small enough to fit into your jar. The more surface area your herbs have, the better the oil will absorb their properties. Make sure to put your intention for opening your third eye and becoming more intuitive into each herb.

Place all your herbs into your jar. Add in your crystals. Top off the jar with olive oil. Close the jar. Anoint your candle with enhancement oil if you've made it. You can also carve some symbols that represent intuition to you. Place this on the lid of your jar, and burn it down. Let your oil sit for a full moon cycle before using it.

DISPEL DOUBT WITH
LEMON PEEL

Fear, worry, anxiety and doubt can hold you back from so much in life. These feelings can also be a big setback when it comes to working spells. If you doubt yourself or doubt the idea that you can have anything you desire, then it can slow down a spell or even keep it from working. Let go of any fear or worry that your dreams will not manifest. If you can imagine it, you can have it. You don't need to know how it's going to happen, but you must be sure that it will happen. Don't worry about the details. Focus on the big picture—the end result. Whether your spell works in a day, a week, six months or even years, be certain that it is coming in the perfect timing. This spell is perfect to do when you are feeling doubtful or are beginning to let anxiety creep in. Stop it in its tracks with this helpful spell.

ingredients
Several sheets of paper
Scissors
Pen
Small bowl
3 tbsp (18 g) dried lemon peel
3 tbsp (9 g) dried thyme
3 tbsp (10 g) dried rosemary
3 tbsp (6 g) dried sage
3 tbsp (6 g) dried lemon verbena
3 tbsp (9 g) dried lavender
Cauldron, bonfire or fireplace

the ritual

I like to do this spell when I am having doubts. If you have already cast a spell and you keep having negative feelings creeping into your head, give this a try.

Take your sheets of paper and cut them into squares about 3 x 3 inches (7.5 x 7.5 cm). You need enough space to add some of the herbs. On your paper squares, write down any doubts you are having. Write down as many as you can think of. Anything you think could go wrong. If you are hung up on the idea of there being limitations, write those limitations down. Any fears, any worries—write them down. Once you have every possible fear written down, set them to the side.

In your bowl, add your herbs one by one and enchant them. As you hold each herb imagine feeling confident, victorious and happy. You now have your desire. You no longer fear anything. Feel positive and self-assured. You are capable of achieving anything you desire in life. Once you have all the herbs in the bowl, mix them together.

Take each paper square and place a pinch of the herb mixture in the center. Fold the paper into little pouches.

Light a small fire in your cauldron. Or if you want to do this outdoors, make a small bonfire. I've done this at the beach several times; it feels amazing to leave your worries behind somewhere else outside your home. Do whatever feels right to you. Take each pouch and throw it into the fire. As you watch the pouches burn, imagine the worries burning away. They are no longer an issue.

Once you are done, toss the ashes away and forget about it. You are now lighter and free to move forward, and your desires will manifest exactly as you wish.

LEMONGRASS ENCHANTED NECKLACE

Lemongrass is known for its ability to empower the energy of spells, and it grants its wearer with the same power. It also aids with concentration, helps clear the mind and strengthens psychic ability. In this necklace, you will be combining herbs with knot magic. Knot magic is simple, but powerful. You can wear this necklace every day or just during rituals. If you prefer, you can also wrap it around your wrist as a bracelet. If wearing jewelry isn't your thing, you can simply hold it in your hand during rituals, carry it in your pocket or keep it on your altar.

ingredients
1 (72-inch [182-cm]) piece of red cord
Sandalwood Spell Success Incense (page 158)
3 fresh lemongrass strands
1 star anise

the ritual

Choose a red cord made of natural fibers. You can use red wool yarn, cotton embroidery thread or anything non-synthetic. You also want to choose a cord that's not too thick so that you can braid it easily. Cut the cord into three 24-inch (about 61-cm) pieces.

Light your incense. Take your cut cords and lemongrass, and pass them through the smoke of the incense. Focus on bringing in strength and determination. Feel yourself empowered and vibrating with energy both mentally and physically.

Tie the herbs and cord together on one end. Begin to braid them together focusing on your intention. Tie off the remaining end. You will be tying seven knots into the cord. Space them as evenly as you can through the length of the cord.

As you tie each knot, say each of these phrases one by one:

With this knot I grant myself inner strength
With this knot I grant myself a strong will
With this knot I grant myself strength and power
With this knot I grant myself psychic vision
With this knot I grant myself a clear mind
With this knot I grant myself focus and concentration
With this knot I grant myself magical ability

String the star anise onto your cord like a pendent. Now it is ready to wear or carry with you.

ROSE PETAL
SELF-COMPASSION SPELL

Having compassion for yourself is not something that comes as easily as you might think. Many times we are working hard and focused on helping others, and we forget about our own physical and spiritual well-being. We might dwell on past mistakes, and it's hard to move forward when we hold on to so much. This ritual helps you forgive yourself for whatever you regret. This can sometimes be a first step toward manifesting your other desires. Part of loving yourself includes forgiveness. So if you feel like your other spells aren't budging or are stuck somehow, this might be what you need.

ingredients
2 pieces of paper
Pen
Pinch of pink rose petals
1 rose quartz stone
1 jade stone
Small pink pouch

the ritual

On the first sheet of paper, write down everything you want to forgive yourself for. If it's one specific situation, write down all your regrets surrounding this issue. Let everything out. Writing is a great healer. If you want to, write down what you wish you had said or what you want to say to a specific person. Sit with your eyes closed and meditate on the situation. Let yourself get angry, cry, whatever emotions come to you.

When you feel ready, take the paper and rip it into pieces. Imagine all those situations ending in peace. You can re-create scenes in your mind and see them as all now ending in love and harmony. Let go of all your frustration and anger. It's all gone now.

Once you feel back in the present moment, write these words on your second piece of paper:

I forgive myself
For all wrongs I have done
Let love fill my being
And let go of the past
I am now whole
I am now filled with love
I exude loving light from above

Set your rose petals and crystals in front of you. Say these words aloud three times over them. Really feel yourself letting go of the past and filling your present life with love for yourself. Feel calm, at ease and at peace. You can even hold the crystals in your hand as you say this.

Place the rose petals on your paper and fold the paper up into a small square. Place the crystals and the paper square in your pouch. Keep this with you.

When you feel yourself repeating negative scenarios in your head, hold the pouch in your hands and feel the gentle energies of these stones. Once you feel like you have fully let go and forgiven yourself you can dispose of the paper square and place the crystals around your home.

CATNIP SELF-GROWTH SPELL

Catnip is a fantastic herb for love and happiness spells, but it is also an ancient magical herb associated with self-growth. If you want to get rid of a bad habit it is said you should burn catnip and dragon's blood. Overcoming an addiction of any kind is extremely powerful. You really show yourself how resilient and strong you are to come out of the depths of darkness. This spell can be used to let go of any negative bad habit or addiction. It allows you to release what is no longer serving you and move forward with tenacity and strength. Do this spell during a waning moon.

ingredients
Mortar and pestle
1 tbsp (2 g) dried catnip
1 tbsp (7 g) dragon's blood
1 tbsp (7 g) frankincense
1 tbsp (6 g) allspice
Charcoal disc
1 (12-inch [30-cm]) piece of black cord
Black tourmaline crystal
Boline or knife
1 black candle

the ritual

Using your mortar, grind the herbs until they become small-sized pieces. Take a pinch of the mixture and light it on your charcoal disc.

Relax, and meditate on what you want to release for 5 to 10 minutes. You can hold the cord and crystal in your hand while you do this.

Using your boline or a sharp instrument, carve what you want to let go of on the candle. If it is many things, write them all, but try to focus on only a handful. Pass your candle through the smoke. Light the candle.

Take your black cord, and tie a knot for every addiction or bad habit. Really do it with force. You want to put all your energy into the knots. Once your knots are finished, take your cord and hold it over the candle's flame until it burns.

Say these words aloud:

> *Burn away this cord*
> *My addictions and bad habits*
> *No longer control me*
> *They are gone and I am free*

Place your black tourmaline next to the candle so it charges. It will absorb all the negative energy and thoughts from your mind. Let the candle burn down.

Carry this stone with you. When you find your mind wandering to thoughts of these bad habits, rub the stone.

DON'T GIVE UP
BAY LAUREL SPELL

Sometimes when things don't manifest as quickly as you would like, you feel like giving up. You start to think maybe magic doesn't work. But you have total control over your thoughts. Your thoughts and intentions are what create the world around you. Often you will get signs that you are on the right path—that things are going in the direction of your dreams. One morning I was driving to get a coffee, and I was having extreme doubt and replaying negative thoughts in my head. I was overthinking things and letting anxiety set in. Then I looked over to the car next to me and I saw their vanity plate: it read DNTGVUP. It made me laugh and all those anxieties dissipated. The universe was telling me not to give up. If you are feeling like giving up, don't despair. Try this spell to boost your belief in magic. Heck, to boost your belief in yourself!

ingredients
Frankincense Power Enhancement Oil (page 146)
1 yellow candle
1 bay leaf
Marker
Heatproof plate or bowl

the ritual

Giving up can sometimes mean giving it up to the magic of the universe. Think about times when you try hard to do something and you get really stressed out, and then as you begin to relax things just start to flow in. This is the idea behind this spell. Bay laurel leaves are often used to "give up" or send out intentions into the ether. So this spell couldn't be any simpler.

Start out by rubbing your oil on your hands. Rub a few drops of oil on the candle. Light your candle.

Write down your intention on the bay leaf in a few words or less. Make this simple, don't get wordy. Really focus on it and put in as much emotion and excitement as you can for its arrival.

Using the candle's flame, light the tip of the bay leaf and let it burn on your plate. Watch the smoke as it carries your wishes up into the air. Leave it up to the universe to act on your behalf. All you have to do now is wait. What you desire is on its way.

PREPARING YOUR TOOLS

Tools are not mandatory but most witches who have been practicing for a long time do have a collection of special tools they use during rituals. For the purposes of this book, fancy tools would be excessive, but they are something you might like to have. There's something special about finding the perfect brass chalice at a thrift store, or inheriting your grandmother's antique silver bowl for your altar that creates an otherworldly atmosphere. Part of the purpose of using tools is that you are creating an altered state in your circle where you will be working with energies. The tools help you set the mood and prepare the space.

Just as you might cleanse your crystals under running water, or through a pass of smoke, you can also consecrate your tools by the four elements. When you set up your altar, you should always have a representation for earth, air, fire and water, corresponding with salt, incense, candle flame and water. Take each tool and sprinkle it with salt, pass it through the incense smoke, through the candle flame and sprinkle it with water. As you pass your tool through each element, you can say these words:

I charge this (name of tool)
By the element of earth (sprinkle with salt)
By the element of air (pass through incense smoke)
By the element of fire (pass through flame)
And by the element of water (sprinkle with water)

This (name of tool) is now charged with the powers of the universe to aid me in my magical workings. So mote it be.

Your tools are now charged to be used for sole use in magical rites. You should be using these tools only for magical purposes. Once you use them you may cleanse them at the end of a spell by simply passing them through smoke. Also make sure to do this with any crystals before you reuse them for any other purpose. You want to discharge any energy used for a specific ritual so that it can be used at a later time.

I have also created a consecration oil you can use on your tools each time you use them. Consecration only needs to be done once, in a formal way, but some people enjoy charging them every time they do a ritual.

To use this oil, you dab some oil on the tool using your finger. This needs to be only the tiniest bit of oil. You can also form a pentagram on the tool using your finger as well. Focus your energy on what you will be using each tool for. Now your tools are ready.

CONSECRATION OIL

ingredients

Mortar and pestle

1 tbsp (3 g) dried rosemary

1 tbsp (3 g) dried lavender

1 bay leaf

1 tbsp (6 g) copal

1 tbsp (7 g) frankincense

1 tbsp (6 g) dried lemon peel

Small jar

½ cup (120 ml) sunflower or other plant-based oil

Using your mortar and pestle, grind the rosemary and lavender. The other herbs can be used in their whole form, as they won't pulverize as well. I also enjoy seeing some whole herbs in the jar as opposed to a murky powdery oil. Place all the herbs into a small jar. Pour the oil over the top. Make sure all the herbs are fully covered. Let this sit for one full moon cycle before using it.

DAY OF THE WEEK REFERENCES

The days of the week and time of day are important when doing spells. Of course you can do spells at any time, but they carry the most energy when they are done on their corresponding day and time. If you are in situation where you need to do the spell right away, or you don't have the privacy to do the spell at that specific time, go ahead and do it whenever. Remember, there are spells that require you to light a candle for several days in a row. So if you do that spell at 10 p.m., make sure to do it around the same time for the remainder of that spell.

Sunday is ruled by the sun. This is a good day to do wealth and career spells. Anything to do with success in business or prosperity.

Monday is ruled by the moon. The moon is a feminine energy, so Monday is also known as the day of women's mysteries. Anything relating to emotions can be done on this day. Also spells of beauty, dreams and wisdom. Matters relating to home and family also can be done on this day.

Tuesday is ruled by Mars. Anything relating to personal power, vitality, success, strength and courage.

Wednesday is ruled by Mercury. This is the day to do spells for communication, divination, self-improvement and change in your life.

Thursday is ruled by Jupiter. This is a good day to focus on healing and health spells. Jupiter rules manifestations of money, love and luck so you can also do money spells or good luck spells on this day.

Friday is ruled by Venus. This is the best day for love, romance and passion.

Saturday is ruled by Saturn. This day is for banishing, cleansing and learning to set boundaries. Saturday is also the day to do protection spells.

LUNAR REFERENCES

During the full moon (also known as esbats) focus on spells that draw things to you or help you gain something, such as abundance, love or health. This is the time to manifest. Many see this phase of the moon as being at its most potent, so anything to do with something coming to fruition or really working with the lunar energy should be done on the full moon. This is also a great day to cleanse your crystals and tools under the light of the moon. You can infuse any oils or other potions you have made on this day.

Many spells also call for you to partake when the moon is waxing. Much like the full moon, you will be focusing on spells that are attracting things to you. Things you want to hold on to or bring into your life.

During the new moon you want to focus on spells where you want to let go of something. Releasing old habits, negative thought patterns or ill health. This is also a time of new beginnings, growth and new projects.

When the moon is waning or decreasing, you also want to focus on spells to let go of something in your life. Release toxic patterns, addiction or banish things from your life.

For both the new moon and the full moon, the energy is highest three days after. So if you miss the actual day of that lunar phase, you can work with the energies three days before and three days after the new or full moon.

HOW TO ANOINT CANDLES AND OTHER QUESTIONS THAT OFTEN GO UNANSWERED

how do i anoint a candle?

There is no real "wrong" way to anoint a candle, but people have different methods. One common way is to start in the middle. With one hand rub the oil up the candle, and with the other hand rub the oil down the candle. The idea is that you are anointing upwards or "as above" and then anointing down the candle "down below." In essence you are unifying the unseen, divine energy from above and bringing it down into this visible, physical realm. When drawing things toward you, you can also pull the oil toward you, instead of pushing it away. Other people simply rub any which way. Some people even lick their candles! This is a way to really add your own energy into it. Likewise, some people chew a bit of herb and place that into a spell, or take a sip of wine before they add it to a potion. There is no wrong way. Rely on your intuitions and do whatever feels good to you.

how do i enchant my herbs and charge my crystals?

You want to give every single ingredient in your spell energy. The herbs are working for you. Much like you would ask a plant for permission to pick some of its leaves or flowers, you are also asking these herbs to perform a task for you. You are giving them a job to do within the context of your spell. So before you use them in your spell work, you want to program them. You can do this by whispering or chanting words over them. So for a health spell you might say the words "heal me" as you hold them. You can blow your breath over the top of them. You can cup them between your hands and simply focus on your intention. You can also pass the herbs through the smoke of your incense. You can say words aloud or in your head while you work the herbs in your mortar. Some people also draw a protective symbol over their herbs such as a pentagram with the hand. Or you can do a combination of these things. Don't worry, with time you will learn to do things in your own way and what feels natural to you.

You should, likewise, charge your crystals for use in spells. Charging your crystals means you are programming them to work for you in a specific spell. For instance, if you want to use a piece of rose quartz for a love spell, you will need to program it to work for that love spell. To charge the crystal you can hold it up to your third eye, hold it in your palm or up to your heart. Whatever feels good to you. Close your eyes and focus on the purpose of your spell. Focus intently for about a minute. Your crystal is now ready to use. Once you have finished using it you can cleanse it and it can be ready to use for a different purpose later. You can try using this cleansing incense to use on any of your crystals before or after charging them.

crystal cleansing incense

1 part frankincense
1 part dried rosemary
1 part dried sage
1 part dried cedar

Lightly crush herbs in your mortar. Mix them together. Keep them in a jar for future use.

can i recharge a spell?

This is something that is really hard to find information on. Sometimes you might do a spell and nothing happens, or you feel like you simply want to keep adding energy to it. This is a tricky one. I would say that in my opinion, once a spell is done it's done. If it isn't coming to fruition, stop thinking about it. Don't keep asking when it's coming. If you did the work, it will come. Not everything happens at lightning speed. Sometimes you might even need to do more than one spell for your desire to manifest. You can recharge amulets, talismans or even protective jewelry such as a pentagram. This is different than cleansing because you will be adding to the energy. If you have been wearing an amulet and feel the energy has dissipated, you can boost the energy. This method uses only candles, but if you want to add some of the herbs originally used in the spell, that's good too. If you have a protection or consecration oil, you can also dab some on the object.

To recharge:
Place five chime or tealight candles in the shape of a pentagram. Place your object in the center of the candles. You can add a sprinkle of herbs used in that spell. Anoint it with the oil. You can even write a sigil or a phrase on a piece of paper and place it underneath. Focus on what you want the amulet to do. What was the original intent? For love? For protection? Focus on that energy. Let the candles burn all the way down. Now your object is ready to wear or use again.

should i keep my magic a secret?

There always seems to be a bit of a debate on whether you should keep your spell a secret or if you can share it. In more ancient occult practices, there are texts that suggest that you let go of some of your power if you share what you are manifesting. There is also the belief that if you share your spell with people who doubt it, that can interfere with your work. I think that this is for the most part true. Not everyone holds the same beliefs or believes you are capable of manifesting your own reality. Or they may not wish the best for you. I don't like to let people know what I am doing within my practice. People can know that you do magic or that you have a collection of herb jars, but as for the specific work I am doing, that is for me alone to know. I don't think that if you tell someone, it will "spoil" your work, but the doubts of others could creep into your mind, or you might feel as though it's not as powerful. It's kind of like when you blow out your birthday candles. Don't tell anyone the wish or it won't come true? That saying came from somewhere.

clockwise vs. counterclockwise

One of the basic rules in magic involves which way you stir, fold or move. When you want to bring something to you, you always want to move clockwise. You stir clockwise, you turn the paper clockwise, etc. You also want to fold any petitions or paper toward you. If you want to banish something or let go of something, you always want to move counterclockwise or fold papers away from you.

can i substitute ingredients? what if i am missing something and i can't find it?

If a spell calls for six different herbs and you don't have one, then leave it out. This won't ruin your spell. The ingredients are merely tools to help you. So if you want to do one of the spells in this book but you are missing an ingredient, unless it's a two-ingredient spell, you can leave it out, or substitute it. If your intuition is calling you to use another ingredient instead, even better! You are learning to trust yourself and you are starting to create your own spells. That is the whole idea.

If you feel like it's really important to follow the instructions, and have all the right ingredients, that's okay too. I know that might sound confusing, because I just told you it's not important. When it comes down to it, it is what YOU believe. If you believe that it's important, it will become important. If driving or biking to find that exact ingredient makes you feel like you are putting more effort and more energy into doing the spell, then that's fantastic! That's what works for YOU! If it makes you feel more in tune with the plants to grow them, then go outside or to your windowsill and pick a couple of mint leaves. Let them dry and put that much more energy into the process. It is all up to you to make your magic!

using plants and herbs that might be considered poisonous or that aren't listed in the book or other books

The beautiful thing about magic is that you can use any object or plant, even fruit in your work. If you associate a plant with a specific intention, then it has meaning for you. Since this book is meant to contain easy to find herbs and plants, I did not go into depth on other less commonly available plants. But if you grow, or can find, different plants that you associate with love or healing, then go ahead and add those into your spells. Whatever special meaning the plant holds for you, it will add that energy. So while you might not think of orchids, orange blossoms, or guavas and strawberries as love plants, I might. It's all up to you! This is why magic is so amazing!

As for poisonous plants, many witches do use things such as belladonna, angel's-trumpet, hellebore, yew, foxglove, lily of the valley . . . the list goes on. Since you won't be ingesting these plants, they can be used carefully on altars or in spell work that doesn't involve ingestion or rubbing it on your person. But do your research, and handle these plants with caution.

do witches use personal objects, human fluids or animals in their spells?

The thought of using animals in spell work makes me physically ill. Witchcraft does not involve animal sacrifice, although there are magic practices that do. But many witches do use animal bones, fur and bugs in their work. These are all obtained ethically, of course! For example, if you find a dead ladybug, you can use it in luck spells. Cat hair obtained from brushing your cat can be used as well. If you find animal bones on a walk through the forest and you want to put them on your altar or use them in a spell, fantastic! Every animal has a significance. If you feel called to add that to a spell in addition to herbs, go ahead! I have even seen some people use bones from their deceased pets or ashes to act as a guide during magic rituals. It is all based on instinct, and what you might feel called to do. If the idea of using any of these objects doesn't feel good to you, then don't use them.

Personal objects, such as hair and blood, can be used. Did you ever become "blood brothers" with your best friends as kids? Maybe that's not a thing anymore, but I know I did. Blood has been used since ancient times to add power and potency to ritual work. For women, using menstrual blood is considered sacred. Again, this is all on what you feel comfortable with, but know that it isn't scary or dark or anything of that sort. Adding blood to your oil recipes, as part of your magical inks or to charge your magical objects can add a strong energy. I find it very empowering personally.

how do i dispose of spell remnants? what should i throw away? is there a difference when trying to let go of something versus bringing it toward you?

Spell remnants include melted wax, flower petals, herbs, salt, ashes—whatever might be left after your spell is complete. Every kind of spell requires different methods. Generally when you are trying to get rid of something you want to take the remnants as far away from your space as possible. You don't want that energy lingering near you or your home. When you want to bring something toward you, such as love or luck, many times you will keep an object with you or keep it close to your home.

Here is a list of ways you can dispose of your spell remnants. When disposing of remnants, use common sense. Never throw anything that will harm the environment. Don't throw anything that is not considered biodegradable into our bodies of water or into the earth. Don't bury plastic or actual trash. These methods are for throwing food items, herbs, flowers or ashes. If you intuitively feel like you need to throw away a jar from a spell, be responsible. Find a recycling bin.

To Let Go

Bury them far away from your home
Flush them down the toilet
Throw them in the trash away from your home
Send it down a river, stream or any moving body of water
Throw it into the wind
Burn them

To Bring Close

Bury them in your yard or in a potted plant
Keep them as sachets, charms or amulets
Burn them to send your wishes out into the universe

do i need to cast a circle before doing spell work? does this always have to be done?

Casting a circle means you are creating a circle of protection for you during your ritual. You are creating a sacred space in which you will work. You are creating an energy field around you. It can be considered a barrier between the ordinary world and the world of magic. It extends through the physical world we see here and through the astral world. This is a temporary sphere you create in which the energy of your magical workings is amplified. While this is definitely something you should be learning to do, as you practice more and more, it isn't necessarily mandatory every time you want to perform a ritual. If you are doing a quick spell, cleanse the space with an herb bundle or do a quick circle cast without calling on the directional elements. If you are doing your spells in nature, I like to think that is already a sacred space and do not cast a circle. It's up to you and how you feel.

do i need an altar to do my magic on? is there a formal layout i need to follow?

An altar is a sacred space we set up where we can honor the seasons, keep working elements for a spell and keep our magic tools. It can be permanent or temporary. It can be set up and taken down every time you want to perform a ritual, or it can be left all year to have a special place to keep all your witchy elements. You can fill it with flowers, candles and symbols for the different Sabbats throughout the year. I suggest you have a dedicated space in your home where you can always come to do your work. It can be the top of your dresser, a small table or even a single shelf on your wall.

It's important as a witch to have a special place where you can come and feel in tune with nature and your energy. You can keep dried flowers from a walk, your crystal collection, your cleansing herbs, incense, candles—pretty much anything you want related to magic. You don't HAVE to have one. You can perform most of the spells in this book on your kitchen table, in your bedroom or on the living room floor if you want. There is a formal layout that is usually associated more with Wicca, but I prefer a looser interpretation. Use whatever botanical elements, candles and witchy décor that you like and that you feel works with the energies of the spell or of the season.

Altar Incense
1 part frankincense
1 part sandalwood powder
1 part rosemary
1 part copal
1 part rose petals

Place all herbs in your mortar. Powder them and mix them together. Store them in a jar.

REFERENCES

Beyerl, Paul. *The Master Book of Herbalism*. Phoenix Publishing Inc., 1984.

Cunningham, Scott. *Cunningham's Encyclopedia of Magical Herbs*. Llewellyn Publications, 2016.

Cunningham, Scott. *Magical Herbalism: The Secret Craft of the Wise*. Llewellyn Publications, 2002.

Cunningham, Scott, and Kimberly Nightingale. *Wicca: A Guide for the Solitary Practitioner*. Llewellyn Publications, 2017.

Dunwich, Gerina. *The Wicca Garden: A Modern Witch's Book of Magickal and Enchanted Herbs and Plants*. Kensington Publishing Corp., 1996.

Gregg, Susan. *The Complete Illustrated Encyclopedia of Magical Plants*. Fair Winds, 2014.

Illes, Judika. *Encyclopedia of Spirits: The Ultimate Guide to the Magic of Fairies, Genies, Demons, Ghosts, Gods & Goddesses*. HarperOne, 2009.

Kaminski, Patricia, and Richard Katz. *Flower Essence Repertory: A Comprehensive Guide to North American and English Flower Essences for Emotional and Spiritual Well-Being*. Flower Essence Society, 1994.

Kemp, Gillian. *The Love Magic Book Potions for Passion and Recipes for Romance*. Little Brown & Company, 2003.

Moura, Ann. *Green Witchcraft: Folk Magic, Fairy Lore & Herb Craft*. Llewellyn Publications, 2009.

Moura, Ann. *Grimoire for the Green Witch*. Llewellyn Publications, 2003.

Penry, Tylluan. *Knot Magic*. The Wolfenhowle Press, 2015.

Penry, Tylluan. *The Magical Properties of Plants (and How to Find Them)*. Capall Bann, 2009.

Radin, Dean. *Real Magic: Ancient Wisdom, Modern Science, and a Guide to the Secret Power of the Universe*. Harmony Books, 2018.

RavenWolf, Silver. *Silver's Spells for Abundance*. Llewellyn Publications, 2009.

Sams, Tina, and Maryanne Schwartz. *Making Your Own Incense*. Storey Books, 1999.

Smith, David. *Quantum Sorcery: The Science of Chaos Magic*. Megalithica Books, 2009.

Smith, Steven R. *Wylundt's Book of Incense: A Magical Primer*. Redwheel/Weiser, 1996.

Telesco, Patricia. *Floral Grimoire: Plant Charms, Spells, Recipes & Rituals*. Ingram International Inc., 2001.

Weinstein, Marion. *Earth Magic: A Dianic Book of Shadow*. Earth Magic Productions, 1998.

Wood, Matthew. *Book of Herbal Wisdom: Using Plants as Medicines*. Atlantic, 1997.

ACKNOWLEDGMENTS

To the amazing team at Page Street for allowing me to write my second book, this is a dream come true. I couldn't have done this without your support and guidance. A special thank you to Lauren, who helped guide me through the process and believed in me so that I could make this book happen. To Jenna, who made the editing process so easy and fun and who was able to turn my ramblings into something cohesive and easy to understand. To Kylie, thank you for your amazing design skills and for putting together such a beautiful book.

To all the witches in my family, and to all my ancestors before me that practiced magic and herbalism. To all my aunts, especially Mely and Martha who share a love of the occult and the metaphysical and who have passed down their stories and experiences. They opened me up to the world of brujería and took me to my first ever limpia. Without them several of these spells would not exist in this book. To Maria, for sharing your wisdom and your family rituals that also helped inspire some of these spells.

To my parents and friends for being extremely supportive. Thank you to my mom, for assisting in the procurement of many of the herbs and plants needed to get this book done. For acting as an assistant during many of the shoots, I couldn't have done it without you!

To my dad, for the constant advice and encouragement throughout the process of writing this book.

To my Aquarius sister Lyndsey, for sharing our journey as young witches doing spells together, even though we now live across the country. It all started with a forest, some sheer fabric, candles and the ranger busting in on our ritual.

To Ines, for helping me throughout the process of writing this book and braving the elements to find the herbs and plants needed for many of the photos in this book. Thank you for playing assistant in many of the photo shoots. Without your help, and your strong arms, many of these bath shoots would be without candles! Your lavender tattoo is a testament to our friendship and the adventures we had throughout the process of this book!

To Lauren, who delved into the witchy world with me selling flower "perfume" door to door and being forced—probably one too many times—into watching *The Craft* and reenacting it with me. You are all so wonderful and without you my life would be incomplete.

To Keys Creek Lavender Farm for allowing me to use their beautiful outdoor bathtub for the photos within the book.

Thank you to everyone for your part in making this all happen. This is truly a childhood dream come true. Blessed be.

ABOUT THE AUTHOR

Ally Sands is the founder of Aquarian Soul, the original crystal-infused apothecary. She has been a solitary green witch for more than twenty years. She is a master herbalist, aromatherapist and reiki healer. She is the author of *Herbs and Crystals DIY: Use Plant Medicine and Crystal Energy to Heal the Mind and Body*. She currently lives in a house full of crystals and herbs with her cat familiar, Sage.

INDEX